To Chris
with love from Mum
Have the best
birthday ever
+ many more.

The Aboriginals

MAKING AUSTRALIAN SOCIETY
Series Editor: D. O'Keefe

The Aboriginals

LEN FOX

NELSON

Thomas Nelson (Australia) Limited
19-39 Jeffcott Street West Melbourne Australia
First Published 1978
Grateful acknowledgement for permission to reproduce illustrations is made to the Department of Aboriginal Affairs, the National Library, Canberra; the Mitchell Library, Sydney; the cover is reproduced by permission of the Aboriginal Arts Council.
Copyright © Daniel O'Keefe Publications, 1978

Fox, Leonard Phillips.
   The Aboriginals.
   (Making Australian Society).
   Index.
   ISBN 0 17 005155 2.
   [1.] Aborigines, Australian. I. Title. (Series).

The author would like to express his indebtedness to a number of research workers and writers, and in particular to Alex Barlow and Marji Hill of the Australian Institute of Aboriginal Studies, and Ted Egan of Aboriginal Artists Agency Limited for advice and criticism.

Printed by Times Printers Sdn Bhd. Singapore
Produced for Thomas Nelson by
DOK Publications, 10 Vincent Street Balmain East 2041

Contents

Part One — THE ABORIGINAL WAY OF LIFE

The First Australians	8
The Aboriginal Life-Style	14
Aboriginal Skills and Crafts	24
Games and Names	32

Part Two — CLASH OF CIVILISATIONS

The British Penetration	37
Land-Taking and Resistance	43
Government Policies	52
Smoothing the Dying Pillow	57
New Waves of Protest	61
Albert Namatjira	67
Federal Advancement Council	71
Some Outstanding Aboriginals	76

Part Three — ABORIGINALS TODAY

A Multi-Racial Society	81
Land Rights	89
Commonwealth Programmes	93
New Aboriginal Bodies	99
The Future	106
Follow-up Activities	110
Index	111

Foreword

by (The Hon.) A. J. Grassby
Commissioner for
Community Relations

Australia is one of the most cosmopolitan countries in the world. It is the product of crossbred vigour and has the best opportunity to build a successful multi-cultural society of any country on earth.

The history of Australia is the history of people from every part of the world yet up until now Australia's history has been written as if the pioneering was done by governors, admirals and peers with often nary a word about the people, their hopes, fears, sufferings and triumphs.

One of the biggest obstacles to the building of a united family of the Australian nation is the perpetuation of the belief that Australia was up until World War II a homogeneous society.

This harmful myth has been used and is used even today to divide the community into 'them' and 'us'. In this context the 'us' are those who were born in Australia in pre-war days or the children of those who were born in Australia in pre-war days. The 'them' comprises post World War II migrants, their children and their grandchildren. A demographic examination of Australia from the earliest days of settlement indicates that it has never been a homogeneous society and Australians—that is those constituting the residents of Australia—have never been homogeneous in the sense of a society predominantly of one nation or ethnic background.

Australia today is one of the most cosmopolitan nations in the world. Australians are drawn from more than 100 different ethnic backgrounds. The Australian workforce is the largest overseas-born workforce in the world outside Israel. The majority of Australian classrooms reflect the multi-cultural and poly-ethnic nature of the society.

As a result of these great changes in the population, Melbourne now has the third largest Greek-speaking community of any city in the world. Italian origin Australians numbering more than one million rank third after the English and the Irish. One-third of all the school children in South Australia are the products of post-war migration. One-third of all the children in Victoria in primary school have a first language other than English and fifty percent of all the primary school children in three-quarters of Sydney are the products of post-war migration.

Australians are the newest people in the world. Forty percent are the product of post-war migration and the median age is twenty-six, so those alive in Australia at the time of World War II are in a minority.

What will the Australian of the year 2000 be like? In my *Credo for a Nation* address at the Sydney Opera House on 9 June 1974, I said this:—

> He will be knowledgeable about the history and heritage of his country. He will be outward looking, and will have a keen awareness of Australia's place in the world and, in particular, its place in the region of the world in which we live. He will be at least bi-lingual and possibly multi-lingual and thereby heir to the full richness of mankind's past. He will no longer speak of the 'Far East', with all the emotional isolation which such phrases imply. And he will no longer walk in the shadows of colonial history.

It is against this background that I warmly commend this series of books on migrants in Australia. They have set out to introduce one Australian to another. They show the richness of the heritage drawn from countries as different as Britain and China, Ireland, Greece and Italy, and, of course, tell some of the story of the Aboriginal people who held Australia in peace and balance for 40,000 years.

It is an exciting series which will bring a great range of fascinating fact to us all. Together the series forms a tribute to Australian people and contributes in a significant way to the development of a multi-cultural and a poly-ethnic society which may yet be an example of unity and amity to many older nations. Above all, the series helps us all to understand the essential fact that an Australian can be John, Giovanni, Dimitri, Johan, Jean, Ivan, Jovan, Sean or Juan.

All are equal, all are Australian and none has the right to deny the other his Australian identity.

(*The Hon.*) *A. J. GRASSBY, Commissioner for Community Relations*

Part One — THE ABORIGINAL WAY OF LIFE

The First Australians

> 'These people are the real—the first—Australians.'
> —Ronald and Catherine Berndt

The story of the Australian Aboriginals is so interesting that thousands of books have been written about it. It is so complex that all that this present book will be able to do will be to give you a few glimpses, state a few facts, suggest what are the main questions to be answered—and leave you to answer these questions yourself.

First, what is the meaning of the words Aboriginal and Aborigine? According to the dictionaries, aborigines (with a small 'a') are the first inhabitants of a country, or at least those found living in that country when the first Europeans arrived. The word comes from two Latin words *ab origine*, meaning from the beginning. An example of the use of the word in this general sense is the sentence: 'The aborigines in North America are known as American Indians.' Older dictionaries used to say that the singular should be 'aboriginal' while the plural could be either 'aborigines' or 'aboriginals'. Today some dictionaries accept either 'aboriginal' or 'aborigine' as the singular.

But that is not all. In Australia there is no widely accepted name for the aboriginals; they are called Aboriginals; and since this word has now become the name of a particular people it is usually spelt with a capital 'A'. The words 'Aborigines' and 'Aboriginals' are both correct, but the Australian Government Style Manual has recently expressed a preference for 'Aboriginals'.

All this may seem to be just a matter of words—but it is more than that. The origin of the word is a reminder that Aboriginals are the original Australians, who have been here far longer than any of the

Tribal elder, Alice Springs

rest of us. They can claim to be the real Australians, while the rest of us are migrants or descendants of migrants. They can claim that to be an Aboriginal is something to be proud of.

This pride has expressed itself in a number of ways in recent years. One has been an attempt to find an Aboriginal word which can be used as a name for Australian Aboriginals. One suggestion is Coorie—sometimes spelt Koorie or Koori. Others are Murri, Marngu, Nunga, Wongai and Yolngu.

Another sign of Aboriginal pride has been that many people whose descent is partly Aboriginal and partly European have proclaimed themselves as Aboriginals. In line with this, the official definition has been simplified so that an Aboriginal is 'a person of Aboriginal descent who identifies as an Aboriginal and is accepted as such by the community in which he lives'. This does away with the use of such words as 'half-caste' or 'mixed-blood' which many people found objectionable. It means that Aboriginals are a vast section of the Australian community ranging from large numbers who retain their traditional customs and languages to many thousands in country towns and capital cities whose way of life in many ways is indistinguishable from that of other Australians.

In these first few chapters we will look at Aboriginals as they were when the white man first came to Australia. It is important to remember that while their way of life has been changed by the coming of the white man, and in most parts completely ended, it still continues today in its basic principles over large areas for large numbers of people. In some areas there has been a revival of interest in traditional ceremonial matters, and ceremonies hundreds of years old are being revived and reinforced.

Aboriginals differ considerably one from another, as do other peoples, but they have certain general characteristics. One writer has described them as 'typically of medium height, with slender limbs, heavy eyebrows, deep-set brown eyes, wide nostrils, a long head and a somewhat protruding lower face. Pigmentation ranges from light tan to dark brown and almost black, while hair is dark brown and grades from straight through wavy to curly'.

Sometimes in this book we will refer to Aboriginal and non-Aboriginal Australians as 'blacks' and 'whites', but 'dark brown' and 'lighter brown'

An untitled painting of an Aboriginal corroboree, probably painted between 1854 and 1863, possibly by S. T. Gill

would be more accurate—especially if the non-Aboriginal has been down at the beach 'getting a tan'.

Where did Aboriginals come from, and when? Some of the theories on these questions have been changed in recent years, but it is generally agreed that they came from the lands to the north, crossing the sea straits which separated these lands from Australia and New Guinea in some form of sea-going craft. It is believed that this took place at least 40,000 years ago, during the last Ice Age, when New Guinea, the Australian mainland and Tasmania were one land mass. Just compare this with the length of time that the white man has been in Australia.

If the length of a stick one metre long is taken to represent 40,000 years, then each centimetre will represent 400 years, and the small

Northern Territory Aboriginals dressed for dancing in 1891

distance of half a centimetre at one end will represent the 200 years of time that the white man has been here.

As Aboriginals spread southward across the continent, they encountered many different kinds of country. Because of these differences, and because they did not have modern means of transport and communication such as railways, motor roads, telephones, radio and television, they lived not as one complete nation but as a number of groups, each living in its own area. The languages of these groups and the way in which they lived were not always the same.

The largest of these groups were known as a tribe, but these were not as tightly organised nor as important as tribes in other countries. The tribe was made up of smaller groups, sometimes called bands or clans. A few families would generally join together in the search for food. Each tribe had its own language or dialect. Some words would be the same in different languages, but other words would be different. Where food was plentiful, a group would have a small area of land on which it sought food, and the tribal area would be small. Where food was scarcer the tribal and group areas would be larger. On the Australian mainland there were probably about 500 or 600 tribes. These varied in size from about 100 to perhaps 1500, averaging about 500. It is estimated that the total population was probably about 250,000 or 300,000, although some authorities put the figure much higher.

Neighbouring tribes would sometimes meet together, and there were contacts for trade and passing on of news, but in the main the different groups lived their own lives. There was nothing corresponding to what we have today in the form of a national parliament or a national army to defend against invasion.

The Aboriginal Life-Style

> 'Perhaps we're only learning now what the Aboriginals have known for tens of thousands of years—you have to go with this country—not against it.'
> —Television commentator Bill Peach

In other continents, people down through the centuries got hold of crops like wheat or rice or maize, and animals like cows or sheep, and learnt how to get their food by digging and tending gardens (agriculture), or by caring for herds of animals (pastoral pursuits), or both. Each of these usually enabled people to settle in the one spot where they would build houses, often forming villages where a considerable number of people would live together.

But Australian Aboriginals developed a different way of life, a way based on *food gathering*—the word 'gathering' being used to include hunting with weapons, fishing, and the gathering of fruits and vegetables from the plants where they naturally grow. One reason that has been given for this is that plants like wheat and animals such as sheep were not available in Australia. But there is some evidence that even when Aboriginals could have got plants suitable for crops from lands to the north, they preferred not to do so, because they saw that in their environment food gathering was a better way of living.

When the white man came to Australia, he found it difficult to get food in the Australian bush, and this helped to lead to a belief that Aboriginal food-gathering meant much drudgery and a poor diet. This was not so. The methods used were varied and interesting, and gave the people involved a chance to show their prowess. And the diet in the main—there were problems of course in drought periods—was a rich and varied one. When W. E. Roth, a Queensland Government official, made a list in 1901 of plants used by North Queensland

The Aboriginal technique of making fire by friction of two pieces of wood

Aboriginals for food, he listed 241 plants whose fruit, berries, seeds, nuts, roots, gum, pods, tubers or blossoms were eaten raw or cooked. This of course was in addition to a rich variety of food from land, sea and river animals.

Similar lists have been given for other areas. Professor Geoffrey Blainey in his recent book *Triumph of the Nomads* writes: 'If we consider the main ingredients of a good standard of living as food, health, shelter and warmth, the average Aboriginal was probably as well off as the average European in 1800 . . . they probably lived in more comfort than nine-tenths of the population of eastern Europe.'

The fact that Aboriginals are food gatherers means that they have to walk from place to place to be where the animals are, or to where the fruit or vegetables are ripe. This means that in general they do not settle in one house or in a village and gather possessions; they move around with as few possessions as possible, and tend to sleep in a temporary shelter for the night or for a few nights. In areas where there is much food in one place, they move about less, and build more permanent shelters.

Because they move around in search of food, Aboriginals have often been called nomads or wanderers. But they are not nomads in the sense that they can wander from one area of land to another and still feel at home. Australia is a land where different regions vary. A food gatherer needs to have a good knowledge of the region, of when and where to find food.

This means that when a group of Aboriginals gather food in a given area, they learn to know the area very well. Their living and thinking is closely tied up with the land's hills and valleys, its rocks and trees and waterholes, its rivers and caves and its birds and beasts.

This is so not only for everyday activities like food gathering. It is so for the deeper thinking of Aboriginals, for their whole way of life, for their religion. Aboriginal religion is closely tied up with the land in many ways. One way is that there are special sacred areas—as sacred to Aboriginals as any church or church ground is to a Christian, and probably even more so. People who have lived with Aboriginals and studied their traditional way of life tell us that to an Aboriginal not only are the special areas sacred, but that he identifies himself with the whole of the land that belongs to his group. To use the words of

The Aboriginal Life-Style

Ronald M. Berndt, 'he has a spiritual affinity with it; it is his very soul, his whole being.'

This closeness to the land, and the fact that Aboriginals do not plough or clear the land, means that they need to preserve nature (the environment) as it is, so that it continues to give food, or to alter it so that it gives more. Here we have an important feature of the Aboriginal way of life which contrasts with that of the white man.

Aboriginal hunting a kangaroo from a painting dated 1857

When the white man came to Australia, one of his main activities was to change the environment, to chop down trees, to kill and perhaps wipe out many of the native animals. It has been said that the motto of many white Australians is: 'If it moves, shoot it; if it doesn't, then chop it down.' This way of thinking is opposite to the Aboriginal way of life, which depends on maintaining the environment, and living in harmony with it without disturbing or upsetting the balance of nature.

The white man felt from the first that his way was better, that he could produce more food from a given area than the Aboriginal. In many parts this was so—because of the white man's knowledge of grains and animals and instruments. But in some of the drier parts of Australia, it soon became clear that the white man's methods had destroyed the waterholes and turned grasslands into desert. In many areas the white man failed, and had to retreat—though the Aboriginal had lived there for many thousands of years.

In recent times more and more people throughout the world are warning that if man continues to change the environment in his present manner, seeking ever-increasing production and power as his goals, and producing ever-increasing quantities of harmful waste products, then he may destroy himself. These people call themselves 'environmentalists' or 'conservationists'. Conservation is recognised by governments and people everywhere as important for the future of mankind. Thousands of years before this happened, Aboriginals were conservationists.

Aboriginals are not merely conservationists in the negative sense that they interfere less with the environment than other peoples. Much of their thinking and acting, whether in religious form or story or dance, reflects a harmony between themselves and nature. Some of their actions have the effect—or are aimed at having the effect—of preserving animals or fruits or making them more plentiful.

These differ in different tribes. Ceremonies are often held which are aimed at increasing the yield of a particular kind of food. A non-Aboriginal onlooker might say that this is just a form of magic that could have no real effect, but the ceremony will strengthen in the minds of the Aboriginals the feeling that they need to live in harmony with nature and to help nature to continue to be bountiful. This could lead to steps to preserve a plant or an animal. Poet Mary Gilmore, who lived close to the Aboriginals when a girl, tells of Aboriginals in New South

The 'Dance of Defiance' from *Australia from Port Macquarie to Moreton Bay*, published in 1845

Wales planting grass seeds and berries, and making fish-balks on the rivers to maintain a food supply in the higher reaches.

T. G. H. Strehlow has described how in one area of Central Australia there were sacred areas or precincts for something like a mile around a sacred cave or other sacred object. Within these sacred precincts all hunting and food gathering was forbidden. These sacred precincts, and watering places where hunting was forbidden, served as sanctuaries to preserve animals in times of drought.

Perhaps the main method used by Aboriginals to make food more plentiful has been the regular burning-off of forest areas. Fire is very important in Aboriginal life. It can be very destructive, but it can be very useful. Early settlers in many areas of Australia noticed how Aboriginals used carefully regulated fires to drive small animals from

Aboriginal hunting ceremony

cover so that they could be killed for food. They also observed that the firing of forest regions got rid of the undergrowth and produced a more open forest, often with a new sweet crop of grass. When the white men found good land suitable for grazing sheep, they often did not realise that this had been prepared by Aboriginal burnings over many years. But Sir Thomas Mitchell in 1848 wrote of 'tracts in the open forest which had become as green as an emerald with the young crop of grass ... thickly imprinted with the feet of kangaroos', and pointed out that this was the result of 'extensive burning by the natives, a work of considerable labor . . . the work is undertaken by the natives to attract these animals to such places'.

Another feature of the Aboriginal way of life which helps to preserve animals is some of their religious thinking. In part this is based on a close kinship between man and animals. This is sometimes called *totemism*, though the totemism of Aboriginals differs from that of people like the American Indians.

The kinship between men and animals is shown in many Aboriginal stories in which a man and an animal seem to be one. For instance, in one story there is a tribe called the Bun-yun Bun-yun who have loud voices and cry out to warn other tribes when a flood is coming down the river. The Bun-yun Bun-yun are men; they are also the frogs who sound a warning by croaking when a flood is likely. Or there is a widow called Deereeree who was frightened at night and used to cry out: 'Deereeree, Deereeree.' She has been changed into the willy wagtail who still cries plaintively: 'Deereeree, Deereeree.'

Again, as an Aboriginal boy or girl grew up he might be told that he had a special link with a particular animal—sometimes more than one animal. He or she would feel an emotional link with this animal and would not (except in special circumstances) kill it or eat it; he would try in general to protect it, and because of his particular totem would have a greater respect for all animal life.

Aboriginal actor Robert Tudawali once told the author that his name means shark, and that he is also of the curlew, goose and turtle totems—giving him a link with four animals. On Melville Island, where he was born, his people, if they heard a curlew call, would say: 'Tudawali must be sick.'

We have seen that the food-gathering life of Aboriginals led them to live in harmony with the land. And since food-gathering is more successful if carried out as a community effort, it led to a life of co-operation. Aboriginals live more as a community than white Australians usually do. Land is not seen as something to be bought and sold by an individual for individual ends; it is part of the life of the whole group. A group will generally act together in gathering food or hunting or fishing, and at the end of the day share the spoils. If there is plenty, then other groups may be invited to share. Sharing is part of the Aboriginal way of life.

The knowledge learned by experience is handed down from generation to generation in the form of religion through story or song or dance or poem or rules of conduct; this knowledge will be mainly in the possession of the older men. When a decision has to be made, it will be made by discussion among the older and more experienced men. The tribe does not have a particular person as king or chief or prime minister. After the white man had come, a practice arose of giving an old Aboriginal (perhaps one of the last of his tribe) a brass plate to hang round his neck with an inscription such as 'Robert, King of Gumbathagang'. This was false—Aboriginals do not have kings.

The Aboriginal sees himself as being related to all other members of his group (which might consist of 100 or 200 persons, or more), and of living in co-operation with them. This feeling in general is stronger than that of a white Australian towards his relations.

This community aspect of Aboriginal life is of special interest today, when many non-Aboriginal people are saying that Western civilisation is based too much on competition and is too much of a 'rat race'. Many white Australians are turning towards community living—Aboriginals have practised community living for thousands of years.

A third aspect of Aboriginal life is that in order to survive, the people have had to develop many skills. These include skill in tracking animals, in making and throwing spears and other weapons, in knowing how to find water, in learning the ways of animals and the seasons when trees and other plants would bear fruit and in knowing how to take food without destroying the source of food. In addition, their life is rich in religion, in stories and songs and poems, in music and dance, in art and handicrafts, and in laws of behaviour which the different groups follow in order to maintain their way of life. On top of all this, as we have pointed out, they have fundamental principles of living without disturbing the environment, and of sharing a community life.

All this means, that though when white men came to Australia many of them dismissed the Aboriginals as 'uncivilised' or 'backward', they were wrong. The Aboriginals had developed a high form of civilisation, well adapted to the land they live in. It had its harsh features of course —every civilisation does. (When the white man came to Australia some of the first things he showed to the Aboriginals were gaols, floggings and hangings.) It lacked much of the scientific and medical

Aboriginal with brass plate

knowledge and technology which other civilisations had developed, and which benifited mankind.

But today, when the values of western civilisation are being so widely queried, there is clearly good reason for respecting the Aboriginal way of life, for studying it closely (this chapter has given only a first glimpse or two), and for being willing to learn from it.

Aboriginal Skills and Crafts

> '... Only a highly civilised race could have survived in such a country, which was probably the most inhospitable continent in the world. His survival over the many difficulties is proof that he is equipped with keen perceptive and mental alertness of a special kind.'
> —Professor Porteous of Honolulu, 1929

It would be nice to show the skills and crafts of Aboriginals by describing 'a typical day in the life of an Aboriginal family.' But just as the environment differs considerably from one part of Australia to another, so does the life of Aboriginals. In addition, there are other differences of custom from one tribe to another which have grown down the centuries.

Some Aboriginal groups live on the coast and are mainly fishermen. Others live in the forest lands and mountains, while others still find a living in the plains of the interior. All these groups have acquired highly developed hunting skills, which can still be seen in Northern or Central areas today—spearing a fish, harpooning a turtle, spearing a wallaby—how many white Australians could do as well?

The efficiency of the spear is often improved by the use of woomeras (or womeras)—specially designed and shaped pieces of wood into which a spear fits so that it may be thrown with greater force and accuracy. A woomera is sometimes used also as a dish, an adze, a fire-making instrument, or a digging instrument. Other weapons include clubs, shields, boomerangs, stone knives and axes and other tools.

The development and use of the boomerang is a striking instance of Aboriginal intelligence and skill. Boomerangs are of several kinds, with

Necklets worn by girls during initiation ceremonies, Melville Island, Northern Territory

two main uses. The non-returning boomerang or killer boomerang is a large, heavy weapon, often with a hooked shape at one end, which is thrown to wound or kill, sometimes bouncing along the ground. The returning boomerang is used by Aboriginals in some parts of Australia only—mainly the east and west. This is mainly a plaything, but it can be thrown into a flock of birds, with a chance of bringing one down—if not, it will return to the thrower. Boomerangs are also sometimes used in music, or in ceremonies.

Aboriginal skill with the boomerang has attracted worldwide attention. In October 1964 a Sydney newspaper reported that Aboriginal boomerang-thrower Joe Timbery from Sydney's La Perouse was earning £100 a week and living in a plush hotel in New York after a seven-weeks tour of Canada and the USA demonstrating his remarkable skill with the boomerang. He was on his way to London and Paris for more successful shows. A simple weapon—but aviation expert Squadron Leader P. J. Rusbridge of the RAAF wrote in the *Sydney Morning Herald* of 15 July, 1974, that when some of his colleagues in a British aviation research establishment attempted to make boomerangs, none of them really worked. He wrote: 'Aerodynamicists may correctly identify all the primary parameters that give the boomerang its lift, manoeuvrability and stability, but they will be lucky to get the values right. But an Aboriginal . . . will certainly get these values right.'

But it would be wrong to suggest that Aboriginal skill in food gathering depends mainly on the boomerang and spear. Only a small proportion of food is got with the boomerang. The spear is more important, particularly at certain seasons and places when large animals are abundant. Very often the women's digging sticks get more food than the men's spears, and the use of both depends on a very deep knowledge—knowledge of animals, how to track and approach them and how to make nets or other snares to catch them—plus knowledge of trees and plants and the right season to visit each. The 'wandering' of Aboriginals is not a casual roaming but a carefully planned programme based on their knowledge of animal and plant, time and season.

Linked with these skills is skill with fire. Aboriginals have the skill to make fire by rubbing wood on wood, either with a sawing motion (perhaps using a hard woomera), or by a fire drill, with kindling from

Aboriginal Skills and Crafts 27

such substance as paperbark, kangaroo dung, or powdered wood dust. They have the skill to keep fire by fire-sticks carried with them (sometimes banksia cones are used). They use fire for many purposes—cooking, hunting, improving pastures, insect repellent, warmth at night, weapon making, beacon for fishermen and smoke signals. Fire, it has been said, is their greatest weapon.

A less important skill, but an interesting one, is the use of poisons. W. E. Roth, who listed 241 plants used by North Queensland Aboriginals for food, also listed twenty-two plants used for getting substances which were used to 'poison' the water of water-holes so that fish would rise to the surface and be captured. Aboriginals also have many devices which enable them to get close to animals without being detected; W. E. Roth tells of North Queensland Aboriginals having a sign language by which they can talk to one another when hunting without

Rock engravings at Mersey Bluff, Devonport, Tasmania

Aboriginal with woomera

alerting the hunted animal. This sign language (sometimes called 'finguistics') is also used for secret talk generally.

Anyone who studies Aboriginal weapons will see that they are not only efficient instruments; they are also usually decorated in a manner which shows great skill in carving or painting. Aboriginals are an artistic people. Their art varies greatly from region to region. In the south-east of Australia, for instance, there were many carved designs on tree-trunks; in the western part of Arnhem Land there are many cave paintings; on parts of the northern coast there are paintings on bark that are not found elsewhere.

When the white man first came to Australia, he tended to dismiss Aboriginal art as 'crude'; today it is highly appreciated. In 1976 the

Australian National Gallery bought 139 bark paintings by the late Aboriginal artist Yirawala, who died earlier in the year at the age of eighty-nine on Croker Island. National Gallery director James Mollison said at the time of the purchase that 'not only was Yirawala an outstanding artist, but his works were eagerly sought after in the United States and much of it had already left the country.'

It was reported that many of these Yirawala paintings are of a sacred nature and should not be shown to everyone. This is a reminder that many of the arts of the Aboriginals—paintings, carvings, stories, songs, dances and music—have a religious meaning, and that the religion of the Aboriginals is something closely bound up with almost everything they do. What appears as 'decoration' of a spear might be seen by the Aboriginal as a form of magic to make the spear more effective; what appears as an amusing story about animals might have a deep meaning.

Some Aboriginal tribes have a story about the first man who died. A spirit with fiery eyes dropped him in the trunk of a white gumtree which soared into the skies followed by two white cockatoos or Mooyi. And today, up near the Warrambool (or flood water) in the sky which white men call the Milky Way, you can see the two eyes of the spirit, and the two eyes of the first man to die; this is called by white men the Southern Cross and by some Aboriginals Yaraan-doo, the place of the white gumtree. What white men call the pointers are really the Mooyi, or white cockatoos, still chasing the gumtree. This story, collected and published by Mrs Langloh Parker, can be seen as just an interesting story, or as an expression of thinking about death by a people who had learnt to see everything in a sense of togetherness—man and animal, earth and sky, life and death.

Other stories, songs and poems of the Aboriginals are more directly religious. Many of them tell of a spirit-world of heroic beings who have left their mark on earth in the form of rocks, paths, waterholes, rivers, lakes and hills. These heroes or gods are seen as living in a time called the 'Dreamtime' or 'Dreaming' which was in the past but is also in the present. All this is part of a very complex religion which differs with different tribes and is difficult to understand.

But we can understand that it would help Aboriginal children to grow up feeling very close to the animals and other natural objects around them, and feeling that there is a spirit-world of beings who have left their mark on earth. They would think of themselves as coming from this world, and going back to it when they die—and this would make an Aboriginal want to live and die in his tribal land, which he would see as being close to his spirit land, to his 'Dreaming'.

Much of the tribe's religious knowledge is not told to the children until they reach a certain age where they are initiated at a special ceremony. At such a ceremony a boy might have a tooth knocked out, or be circumcised, and might have to endure certain tests which prove his courage.

After initiation, an Aboriginal youth is able to marry; but he is not able to choose a wife freely; he has to marry according to certain laws; in fact his whole life is lived according to tribal laws or customs which are often very complex, but which can be seen as helping to preserve the way of life.

If an Aboriginal breaks a major law, he is subject to punishment, just as a member of any other civilised society would be. Sometimes the offender is given more of a chance than many offenders in other societies—he has to stand up in the open, armed only with a shield, and face a barrage of spears thrown at him. Quite an ordeal, but if he dodges or wards off the spears cleverly enough, he may be allowed to go free with only a slight wound or two.

We have not yet, of course, mentioned nearly all the skills and crafts of Aboriginals. From the very first, white men were attracted by the picturesque and spectacular character of Aboriginal dances, particularly the big corroborees where perhaps several tribes might gather together for a ceremonial dance. More recently, it has been realised that Aboriginal dancers are not merely spectacular; experts have said that some Aboriginals are among the finest dancers in the world. American dancers Beth Dean and Victor Carell travelled 10,000 miles to study Aboriginal dancers, and wrote a book about it telling how dancing to Aboriginals is 'a living and vital art that was not merely an occasional amusement but entered into every phase of their life', and that the corroborees they witnessed were 'dignified and full of the highest ideals.'

Many corroborees are sacred dances; others are more everyday, and may deal with modern objects and themes such as aeroplanes. Many years ago one white pioneer in Queensland told of seeing a corroboree where the dancing showed Aboriginals spearing cattle and being attacked by whites for doing so; then the Aboriginals rallied and drove the whites out—to great cheering from the Aboriginal onlookers!

Recently, more interest has been taken in Aboriginal music, and performers like Rolf Harris have popularised the didgeridoo (or dijeridu). This is a hollow piece of wood four or five feet long with a mouthpiece made of wax or hardened gum. Percussion instruments like tapping sticks are also used.

Much more could be written about the skills and crafts and social organisation of Aboriginals, but even a short summary shows that they compare well with those of any other group of people. Such skills were not acquired easily. They are the skills and social structure of people who came to a strange continent that varied from region to region and lacked many of the main plants and animals of other lands.

It was a continent that changed greatly as the seas rose following the end of an Ice Age, so that large areas were swallowed up and climatic conditions in others changed. To discover Australia, to explore it, to know it, to learn how to use its widely varied resources, to build a way of life to suit the changing environment—this was an achievement of which any people could be proud, and it is fitting that Professor Geoffrey Blainey should have called his book telling the history of Aboriginal Australia *Triumph of the Nomads*.

Aboriginals with didgeridoo

Games and Names

I like the native names, as Parramatta,
And Illawarra, and Woolloomooloo;
Nandowra, Woogarora, Bulkomatta,
Tomah, Toongabbie, Mittagong, Meroo;
Buckobble, Cumleroy, and Coolingatta,
The Warragumby, Bargo, Burradoo;
Cookbundoon, Carrabaiga. Wingecarribee,
The Wollondilly, Yurumbon, Bungaribbee.
—Dr John Dunmore Lang, 1824

When Europeans first visited Australia, they took most notice of those parts of Aboriginal life which were different from their own. Aboriginals had a different skin color; they wore fewer clothes, they had spears instead of guns, fire-sticks instead of matches; their houses were different; their dances were different, and so on.

Later on, white observers began to put on record the countless ways in which Aboriginals resemble other peoples. Their intelligence, their love of nature, their warm love of children, their belief in a moral code of behavior, their fondness of story-telling, for art and song, dance and music, their humor . . . Some of the early explorers saw Aboriginals as miserable people, but Captain Cook said in one of his letters: 'In reality, they are far happier than we Europeans . . . The earth and sea of their own accord furnishes them with all things necessary for life. They covet not magnificent houses, household-stuff, etc.; they live in a warm and fine climate, and enjoy every wholesome air, so that they have very little need of clothing; and this they seem to be fully sensible of, for many to whom we gave cloth, etc., left it carelessly upon the sea beach and in the woods, as a thing they had no manner of use for; in short, they seemed to set no value upon anything we gave them . . .'

This happiness expresses itself in many ways; one is in playing games. Some of the games are like games played the world over. Observers

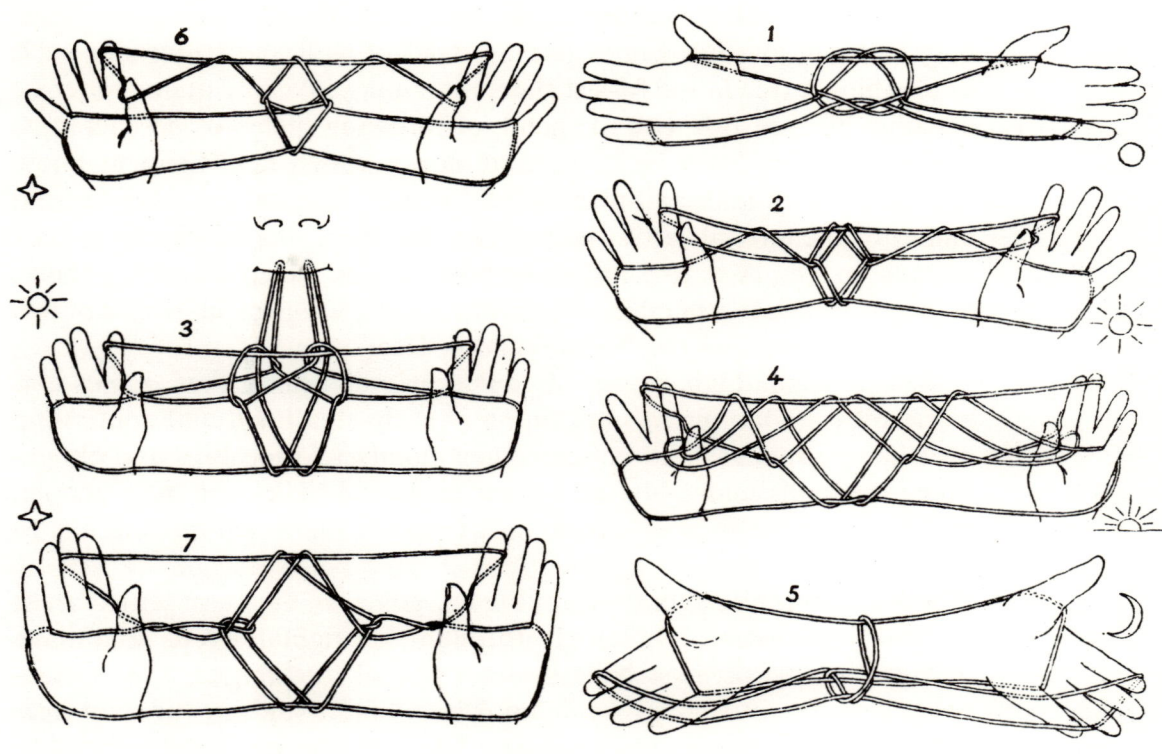

String games played by Cape York children. 1 Sun: clouded over; 2 Sun: full rays; 3 Sun: full rays; 4 Sun: setting; 5 Moon; 6 Star; 7 Star.

down the years have noted that children played hide and seek, swinging on vines, mud slides (men and women enjoyed this too), bathing, splashing, diving, wrestling, telling stories, 'playing grown-ups', and making 'cats' cradles' with fingers and string. Boys played at imitation warfare; in some areas girls had dolls. Adults in some regions played with spinning tops. There were also ball games; 'catching' was played with a ball made of possum or wallaby hide tied with string; there were also games where small spears were thrown at a ball or disc as it rolled along the ground.

Many of the children's games are educational, helping them to know their environment and its animals. For instance they may be asked to track a frog which has been released unseen by the children, or to follow an ant and notice the marks that it leaves. As they grow older they will join in adult games that are tests of skill and endurance such as climbing a tree in the fastest time, remaining invisible under water or catching birds or fish with the hand, or throwing spears or boomerangs.

Children also learn by being told stories which help them to know the names of animals and plants, and to learn their habits. Many of the names of the animals are—as in other countries—based on the sounds animals make. A native turkey or bustard was called Gomble-gubbon by some tribes, the laughing kingfisher Goo-goor-gaga or Kookaburra, the crow Wahn, and the Willy Wagtail, Deereeree.

But Aboriginal education, of course, is much more than games and stories; it is a long process beginning in early childhood and continuing over many years as children learn their family relationships and obligations, the skills and crafts and knowledge and beliefs of their people, and the potentialities of development within one's self in relation to one's people.

Much of the Aboriginal way of life has gone. In the more settled areas we catch glimpses of it largely through Aboriginal words that have survived. Some of these have become part of our language, like billabong, gunyah, kurrajong, galah, coolabah, bindi, yakker, and churinga.

Then there are many place names. The early British settlers tended to name places after kings or queens or governors or dukes or earls. Dr Lang in 1824 wrote the poem from which a verse is quoted at the beginning of this chapter in protest at the number of places named monotonously after Governor Macquarie and Lord Goulburn. ('Goulburn Downs and Goulburn Plains, And Goulburn River and Goulburn Vale! One's brains are turned with Goulburns!') Today we still have countless places and streets named after Goulburn and Macquarie, King George and Queen Victoria. And many people show that, like Dr Lang, they prefer the music of the Aboriginal names, when they give such names to their homes or streets or localities.

It is unfortunate that the meanings of Aboriginal place names are often in considerable doubt. Often a name was recorded without care being taken that it was an accurate rendering of the Aboriginal word; often there was doubt as to the meaning, and often there was no record of which Aboriginal language the word came from. Thus Wollongong is sometimes said to mean 'Hard ground near water', sometimes 'Five islands' (after the islands off the coast near Wollongong), and sometimes 'See, the monster comes'— expressing the feelings of Aboriginals as they saw large sailing ships off the coast.

In spite of this, Aboriginal names hold their attraction, because of their musical sound and because their accepted meanings reflect a love of nature.

A few examples, and their generally accepted meanings, are: ARALUEN—place of the water lily; BALLARAT—camping place; BONDI—sound of tumbling waters; CANBERRA—meeting place; CARCOAR—a frog; ECHUCA—meeting of the waters; GIRRAWEEN—place of flowers; JERILDERIE—reedy place; KEIRA—high mountain; NOWRA—black cockatoo; TARCOOLA—river bend;

These string games depict animals. 1 Water-snake; 2 Snake; 3 Death-adder; 4 Crocodile; 5 Crocodile nest, with egg; 6 Frog; 7 Turtle.

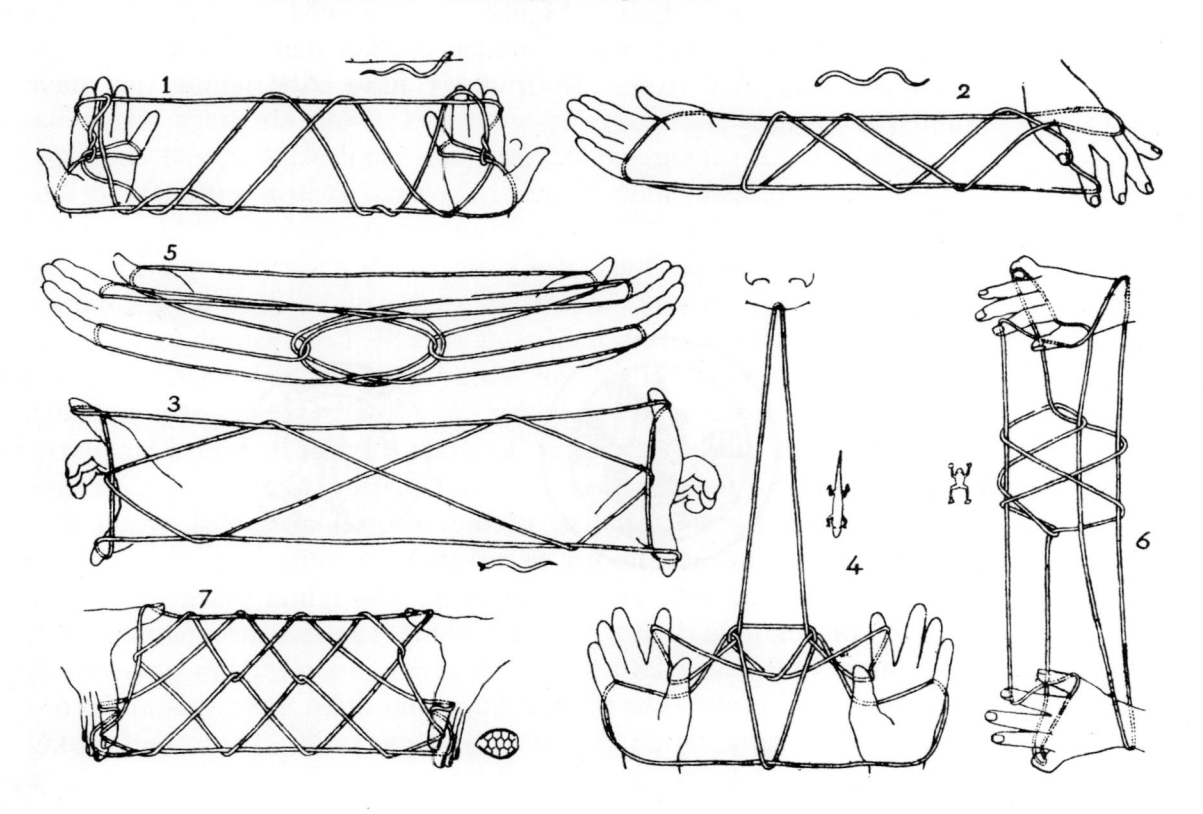

ULLADULLA—safe harbour; WOOLLOOMOOLOO—young kangaroo; WOY WOY—deep water; WAHROONGA—home.

The Aboriginal sense of humor was sometimes shown when a white man would ask the name of a place, and an Aboriginal would answer by giving not the name of the place, but a rude word. The white man would go around repeating this rude word, while the straight-faced Aboriginals would have a good laugh inwardly. Even quite recently it was suggested that 'Moomba', the name for the annual Melbourne Arts Festival which is supposed to mean 'Let's get together and have fun', really means 'bottom' (in the anatomical sense). No one seems to be quite sure!

One final point is interesting. As this book was being written, the Rugby League Final in Sydney was played between Parramatta and Manly. Parramatta is an Aboriginal name whose meaning is usually given as 'Place of Eels' or 'Plenty of Eels', and the Parramatta players are often called the 'Eels'. Manly is so named because in 1788 Governor Phillip noted the 'confidence and manly behaviour' of Aboriginals he met there. Both areas have Aboriginals on their municipal crests.

Council crests featuring Aboriginals

Part Two — CLASH OF CIVILISATIONS

The British Penetration

> 'The Aborigines became trespassers in their own country.'
> —Official Department of Territories booklet *The Australian Aborigines*, 1967

On 29 April, 1970 most Australians celebrated the bicentenary of the landing of Captain Cook as a happy holiday. But Aboriginals from many parts of Australia gathered at Botany Bay for a day of mourning. They wore red headbands to symbolise 'the spilt blood of ancestors', and carried placards with the names of vanished tribes. 'As you celebrate,' said Pastor Doug Nicholls (now Sir Douglas Nicholls), 'we mourn the loss of a great people.'

In 1770, Aboriginals knew that occasionally big ships had appeared off the coasts and strange white-faced men had landed, only to go away again. What the Aboriginals could not know was that in Western Europe a few nations—British, Dutch, Spanish, French, Portuguese, with Germans to come later—had developed industries, weapons, navies, armies— and a growing belief in exploring the world, building empires and enriching themselves by setting up colonies. This has been called *colonialism*.

In this process, the Europeans penetrated vast areas of Asia, America, Africa and Australia. They benefited greatly by plundering precious metals and jewels, by building trade, by finding markets and by securing areas for investment of their money. But the people whose countries were being penetrated (the 'colonial peoples') did not find the process so pleasing. Their lives, they found, were being disrupted in various ways.

In Australia, one of the first of these disruptions became evident as early as 1789. Large numbers of Aboriginals around Sydney were found to be dying of a disease that was apparently smallpox introduced by the white man. Since then, white men's diseases have killed large numbers of Aboriginals. It appears that some diseases which are generally not fatal to whites can be deadly for Aboriginals, because they have not built up an immunity to the illness.

This was serious. But the main disruption to Aboriginal life was a million times more serious than this. The newcomers began to spread out and take up land for sheep farming and other purposes. This act of taking the land and using it for their own purposes struck at the very basis of Aboriginal living. The Aboriginal depended on the land for his food, and when the land was taken his food was taken and with it a basic part of the Aboriginal way of life, of Aboriginal thinking, religion and social structure, was destroyed.

To understand how the Aboriginals must have thought, we should try to imagine how we would feel today if strange beings from outer space, with superior weapons and numbers, poured on to Earth and took over our country, penetrating our homes and churches and most sacred places, preventing us from getting a living in the way we had known, establishing their laws by force of arms, and offering us nothing but an occasional hand-out, and a vague promise that we will find happiness if only we become like the invaders, adopting their religion and way of life.

How did it happen that a nation which prided itself on being Christian and democratic could have acted in a way which meant destruction and death for so many of the First Australians? One reason was that a number of the British who came to Australia had no understanding of Aboriginal society, and believed they could settle in Australia without causing great interference to the original inhabitants. The British Government's instructions to Governor Phillip stated that the whites were to live in amity with the natives, and to be punished for destroying them or for unnecessary interruption of their occupations. Later instructions to Governor Darling stated that he was to protect the native inhabitants and 'the free enjoyment of their possessions.'

But before long it became clear that the only way the white men could ensure that the black men had uninterrupted and free enjoyment of their possessions was to pack up and return to Europe. And before long it became clear that policy towards Aboriginals was decided not by the British Government or the Governor, but by settlers and their servants (many of them convicts or ex-convicts) on the spot. These men saw it as their job to take the land, and to destroy those who resisted. The

Guns against spears—mounted police of last century rout Aboriginals

authorities supported them. More and more they attempted to justify this by asserting that Aboriginals were an inferior race.

Scientists have again and again stated that there is no evidence that any race is superior to any other in mental capacities or temperament. But in Western Europe at the beginning of last century theories of European racial superiority were widespread, and they provided a handy justification for those who were engaged in seizing colonies. Once it was held that a black man was inferior, then it was only another step to thinking of him as less than human—and only another step to killing him. Adolf Hitler was able to use such racist theories in the 1930s to whip up feeling that led to the deaths of millions of people.

The 'Day of Mourning' 29 April 1970. While white Australians celebrated the bicentennary of the landing of Captain Cook, Aboriginals gathered at Botany Bay wearing red head bands. Wreaths were cast in the sea. 'As you celebrate' said Pastor Doug Nicholls (now Sir Douglas Nicholls, pictured at left) 'we mourn the loss of a great people.'

Racism did not always take extreme forms. Sometimes it expressed itself in the statement that black people are likeable, but are like children, unable to make their own decisions—so a white man has to decide everything for them. This is usually called *paternalism*.

Sometimes contempt for the Aboriginal took the form of considering that his culture, his way of life (not the Aboriginal himself) was inferior. This is sometimes called *ethnocentrism*. This was often expressed in a theory that because the Aboriginal had not used metals, he was 'thousands of years behind the white man.' Aboriginals could equally have claimed that because Burke and Wills perished in an environment where Aboriginals could live, the white man's culture was thousands of years behind that of the original Australians.

But the white men persisted in their idea that Aboriginals were 'a backward and low race', and this false idea became widespread and lasted down the years; those very words were used by a respectable Melbourne daily newspaper as late as 1938 in describing Aboriginals.

These racist and ethnocentric ideas were assisted by the use of names which have a contemptuous ring to them, like 'Jackie' or 'abo' or 'coon' or 'boong' or 'nigger'. Even the word 'blackfellow', though sometimes used by Aboriginals themselves, is often used with a contemptuous tone to it. The ideas were also assisted by the use of *stereotypes*. A stereotype, according to the dictionary, is a fixed mental impression. If a person studies athletics results and concludes that Scandinavians are good distance runners but not so good as sprinters, this is a reasonable stereotype. But if he then concludes that every Scandinavian is a good distance runner but poor sprinter, the stereotype becomes unreasonable. And if he sees one drunken Scandinavian and concludes that all Scandinavians are drunks; then this is even more unreasonable. But when white men came to Australia and began seizing the land, they often tried to justify this by such stereotypes, in which all Aboriginals were seen as 'lazy' or 'unreliable' or 'always wanting to go walkabout'. Such stereotypes tend to persist, and today, if an Aboriginal worker leaves a job where conditions are bad, people are likely to say: 'He went walkabout', whereas if a white worker did the same thing people would say: 'He took a commendable stand against bad conditions', or: 'He took a well-earned holiday.'

From 1788 on over many long years, these contemptuous attitudes towards the original Australians played a major part in our history. They were the background to a long series of violent clashes, including many massacres, between two ways of life. What decided the outcome of the clash was not which culture was the higher and better; this was a matter of opinion. What decided the outcome was that the Europeans had superior weapons and the ability to muster superior numbers. This enabled them to make the First Australians trespassers in their own land.

The clash was to be a long and complex one. We will look at some of it in the next chapter.

Before doing that, it should be noted that the coming of white civilisation destroyed Aboriginals in a number of indirect ways, as well as in the taking of land and the introduction of diseases. An example was Bennelong (or Benelong), a fine young Aboriginal who was captured near Sydney by Governor Phillip. Phillip tried to be friends with Bennelong, gave him the best of clothes, food and drink, and took him to England.

Bennelong, probably sensing that white people looked on him as a curiosity and as an inferior, was unhappy in white society, but after his return from England found it difficult to go back to Aboriginal society. He turned to one of the white man's vices—drink—and died when quite young, after becoming a lonely and drunken figure haunting a part of Sydney which became known as Bennelong Point—the site of the present Opera House.

One way or another, over most of the continent the Aboriginal way of life was destroyed. In the words of modern Aboriginal poet Jack Davis:

The tribes are all gone,
The spears are all broken:
Once we had bread here,
You gave us stone.

Land—Taking and Resistance

> '... we were hunted from our ground, shot, poisoned, and had our daughters, sisters and wives taken from us.... They stole our ground where we used to get food, and when we got hungry and took a bit of flour or killed a bullock to eat, they shot us or poisoned us. All they give us now for our land is a blanket once a year.'
> —Old Aboriginal Dalaipi, in Tom Petrie's *Reminiscences of Early Queensland*

Australian history is usually written from the viewpoint of the white man. The words at the beginning of this chapter tell the history of last century from the viewpoint of an Aboriginal.

The clash began quite early. By 1794 David Collins, a Judge-Advocate, was reporting that on the Hawkesbury River a body of Aboriginals had attacked and carried off clothes and provisions, that settlers had followed them and killed seven or eight on the spot. The penalty of seven or eight lives for theft indicates the atmosphere of the time.

Collins added the statement that 'whatever the settlers at the river suffered was entirely brought on them by their own misconduct; there was not a doubt but that many natives had been wantonly fired upon; and when their children, after the flight of their parents, have fallen into the settlers' hands, they have been detained at their huts, notwithstanding the earnest intreaties of their parents to have them restored.'

That the settlers were taking Aboriginal children and refusing to return them shows that the whites were treating the blacks not merely as inferior persons, but as something less than human. Collins himself, while stating that the whites were to blame, wrote that the method of treating Aboriginals (killing seven or eight) 'had become absolutely necessary from the frequency and evil effects of their visits.'

The British Government by 1825, in instructions to Governor Darling, wrote that if 'Plunder by Native Inhabitants' could not be stopped by less vigorous measures, it could become necessary 'to oppose force by force', and to 'repel such Aggressions in the same manner, as if they proceeded from the subjects of any accredited State.' This was a recognition of a state of war in which Aboriginals were being treated not only as trespassers in their own country, but as enemy aliens.

In the early years, when Australia was mainly a prison settlement, only a small proportion of Aboriginal land had been taken. But wool-growing developed rapidly; by 1821 wool was being exported to England, and by the 1830s there was large-scale British investment in Australian wool. Land and wool became the great source of wealth and prestige, and squatters extended their holdings throughout the country. Any humanitarian ideas that Aboriginals had rights to the land took second place to the determination of pastoralists and investors to extend their woolgrowing empire.

How lightly many white settlers thought of killing Aboriginals can be seen in a statement in 1834 by writer W. H. Breton (*Excursions in New South Wales, Western Australia and Van Diemen's Land*) in which he criticises whites who 'consider it a pastime to go out and shoot them' (Aboriginals). While criticising such whites who hunted Aboriginals as though they were wild animals, Breton also wrote: 'In case of any serious affray . . . it . . . would be . . . most judicious . . . to make upon them at once, a strong impression, for if only one or two be killed, the sole effect is to instigate them to revenge their companions, whereby a series of murders on both sides is the consequence.'

As the white settlers spread across Australia, relations between the two races became worse. The situation differed in different parts. In some areas the white man was able to settle without completely destroying the Aboriginal sources of food. There was still the ocean left for the Aboriginals to fish in, or enough open land left for them to hunt on; occasionally the white settler needed some labor which the Aboriginals could supply in return for food. And so, for a time at least, the two groups were able to live together, and the Aboriginals had time to adapt to the new conditions.

But this did not happen in most cases. The general picture was something like this. The taking of the land left the Aboriginals short of food.

An 1855 cartoon from the *Melbourne Punch* shows the Aboriginals being driven from their land so it can be sold to white settlers

Since the white man was killing their animals, it seemed natural to the Aboriginals that they should be entitled to kill one of the white man's animals for food. Their way of life was based on sharing, not on private property, so this seemed a moral thing to do. But when Aboriginals killed a sheep or cow, the white man killed Aboriginals.

The choice for many Aboriginals was slow death because their land, their means of food, and their whole way of life had been taken—or else resistance. Again and again they resisted. They struck back at the invader, attacking his sheep or cattle or stores or the white man himself. It was hopeless. Spears against guns. Often the white man, taking the advice quoted above from Breton, massacred a whole tribe.

Usually the details were not recorded. In theory, the white man could be brought to court and charged with murder, but in practice he was not.

There was one exception to this. In 1838 eleven white men were charged with murder following the killing of twenty-eight Aboriginal men, women and children at a place in New South Wales called Myall Creek. The Aboriginals had been massacred, according to the evidence, not because they had killed whites, but because they were alleged to have made 'depredations' against sheep and to have 'rushed' cattle. (Any stranger can frighten cattle causing them to 'rush' through the bush with possible harmful results.)

The Aboriginals had not been warlike. They had been sheltering in the hut of a friendly white man when the group of whites (mostly convicts assigned to work for settlers) seized all twenty-eight of them, tied them up, and took them to a place where they were all shot or killed by the sword—men, women and children.

White settlers contributed money to help the defence of the arrested men, and newspapers supported them. The *Sydney Herald* (which became the *Sydney Morning Herald*) argued in an editorial that the British had had a perfect right to take possession of Australia 'under the Divine authority, by which man was commanded to go forth and people, and *till* the land.' In other words, because the Aboriginals had not ploughed the land, they had no right to it and were trespassers on the white man's land.

The eleven men were acquitted. But some people protested, in particular a man named Edward Smith Hall who was editor of a paper called the *Monitor*. As a result, a fresh case was brought against the men, and this time seven of them were found guilty and hanged.

But this was only one of many massacres of Aboriginals, both before and after 1838. Generally, no one was punished. Often the killings would not even be reported. Sometimes poisoned flour was used instead of guns and swords. After 1838 the governments began to use special border police in the areas where white settlers were clashing with Aboriginals. These were supposed to be impartial, but since they were there to enforce the white man's law, and since this law allowed whites to shoot the blacks' kangaroos but forbade the blacks to kill the whites' sheep, the police became in the main a weapon—and often a deadly weapon—against the Aboriginals. Massacres were now sometimes carried out by the police, or by police and settlers combined.

When the Aboriginals' bushcraft enabled them to escape in the bush, the white man enlisted Aboriginals (from other tribes) in native police forces, which, first in Victoria and then in New South Wales and Queensland, hunted down the First Australians—Aboriginals being used against Aboriginals.

The Aboriginals fought back—this illustration shows the attack on the Barrow's Creek Telegraph Station in 1874

In the Sydney *Sun* of 2 April, 1970 author Keith Willey wrote: 'As late as the turn of the century, some stockmen took a pride in shooting every Aboriginal they met, regardless of age or sex.'

The massacres continued right into this century. In May 1927 there was a slaughter of probably about twenty-five Aboriginals at Forrest Creek in Western Australia; the Royal Commission report of what happened is not allowed to be freely published. In November 1928 there were press reports in Sydney of the killing of seventeen Aboriginals at Coniston by police from Alice Springs. The Board that was appointed to inquire reported that the number of Aboriginals killed was thirty-one; it exonerated the police; but many people were dissatisfied with the Board's findings, and some say that the death roll was at least eighty.

The Aboriginals continued to resist for years. But because of their lack of guns, because of their small numbers and lack of national or even statewide organisation, their resistance was hopeless. In some other countries, like New Zealand and America, the indigenous people were able to organise such a powerful resistance that the white man had to sign treaties giving the Maoris or Red Indians areas of land—thus giving a sanctuary, and time to adapt. But in Australia the Aboriginal resistance was not powerful enough to win any treaty.

The Aboriginal resistance fighters were brave, and determined. They fought year after year, and occasionally when they got guns they became newspaper headlines. But one after another they were beaten, imprisoned, killed. A young warrior named Dundalli fought for some years in Queensland in the 1840s against whites who were violating a taboo placed by the Aboriginals against the cutting of the bunya pine. He was publicly hanged in Brisbane in 1855. In Western Australia a 'black tracker' named Pigeon killed a policeman and became leader of a group of Aboriginal outlaws; he was shot by police in 1897. In New South Wales Jim Governor, 'black tracker' and cricketer, became an outlaw with his brother Joe; one was shot and the other hanged. Some of the leaders of the resistance of the Maoris and the American Indians have become well known as colourful figures in history and even heroes; the leaders of the Aboriginal resistance have been looked on as pests.

If Aboriginals had been like the people in many other colonial countries, practising agriculture and living in villages, they might have been better off. When the white man penetrated a country where the people were villagers, he was often able to leave the village untouched and to take less important land outside the village where the villagers could work on his plantation; such an economic arrangement allowed the two races to live together for a time at least and each obtain something from the other. But the Aboriginals were not villagers; they were not agriculturists; to them all the land was vitally important, and the coming of the white man meant conflict—and often death.

By 1845 the tribes between Broken Bay (the Hawkesbury) and Botany Bay were nearly extinct, and a man and three women were all that were left of the tribe occupying the southern shores of Sydney Harbor which had numbered about 400 in the time of Governor Macquarie about thirty years earlier.

This old photograph shows Aboriginals in chains as they were seen by Daisy Bates early this century. The practice of chaining Aboriginals continued till the late 1950s and in the Sydney *Sun* of 11 December 1961, a senior police inspector in Darwin was reported as saying that 'he regretted police were no longer allowed to chain Aboriginal prisoners by the neck.' He stated that chaining of witnesses as well as accused 'was common practice in the Northern Territory' despite an order from Canberra in 1940 that chaining of Aboriginals must stop.

Further away from Sydney, more were able to survive, but the official figures for the number of Aboriginals of full descent in New South Wales tell a tragic story:

1788 (estimated)	45,000
1871 (estimated)	13,000
1891	5,097
1901	3,778
1921	1,597
1947	953
1956-57 Welfare Board figure	235

The figures may not be entirely accurate. But the trend is clear. For the whole of Australia the drop was from about 250,000 or 300,000 (estimated, or perhaps more) in 1788 to about 40,000 Aboriginals of full descent by 1960.

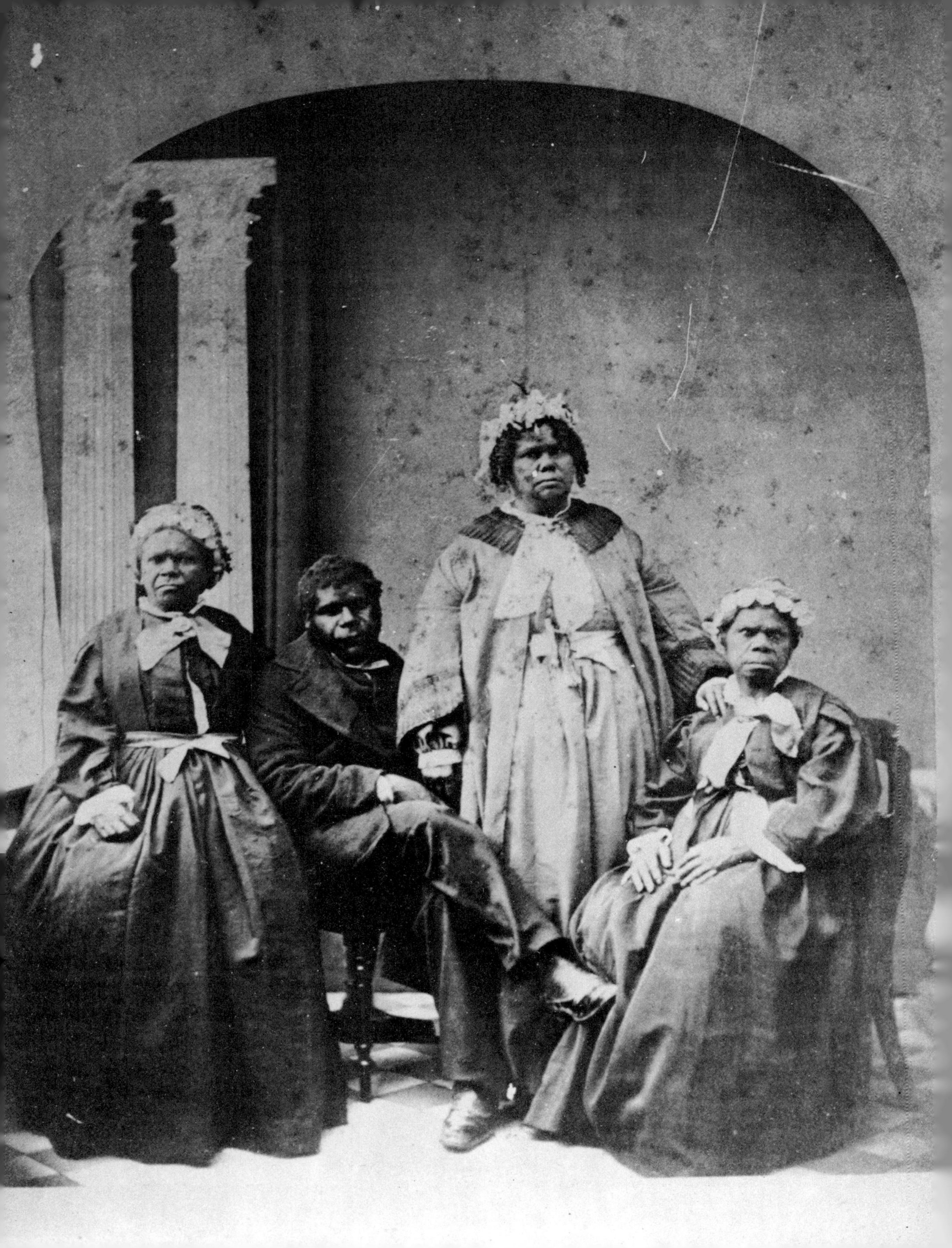

In Tasmania, where the Aboriginals were different in many ways from those on the mainland, the last Aboriginal of full descent died in 1876—less than seventy-five years after the coming of the white man.

Her name was Truganini. She had lived to see her mother, her sister and her intended husband killed or carried off by whites; she had seen the last of her people rounded up and taken to Flinders Island. The last male, William Lanney, aged thirty-four, died in 1869.

Part-Aboriginal descendants of the Tasmanian Aboriginals lived on on Cape Barren Island, held a conference in Launceston in 1971, and today proudly proclaim themselves as Aboriginal people. But the civilization of their ancestors was destroyed a hundred years ago.

(John Batman in 1835 signed an agreement with elders of the Dutigalla tribe giving him about 600,000 acres of land near what is now the city of Melbourne in return for some 'blankets, knives, looking glasses, tomahawks, beads, scissors, flour, &c.' plus a promise of a yearly tribute. The treaty was disallowed by the Government, and Batman was criticised. But in his defence it could be said that at least he did make an agreement with the Aboriginals and did give them something for their land; most white men did neither.)

In the middle of last century, it was common for people to put on their Sunday best clothes and pose for a family photograph. Usually they looked proud and happy. This photograph is different. There is sadness, not happiness, in the faces of these people. And underneath the photograph, in the Mitchell Library collection, are the words: 'The Last of the Tasmanian Natives.' The last Tasmanian Aboriginal of full descent died in 1876, less than seventy-five years after the coming of the white man.

Government Policies

'An old Aboriginal once described Europeans to me in eight words: "Very clever people; very hard people; plenty humbug." '
—W. E. H. Stanner, *Sydney Morning Herald*, 2 May, 1964

White men came to Australia with the idea that Aboriginals were inferior. Alongside this there was generally the equally false idea that Aboriginals would want to become like white men, and would easily adjust their way of life and fit into white society. Since they had these ideas, the early authorities did not feel it was necessary to do anything much about Aboriginals, except to state that they were equals, protected by law. While this was being said, Aboriginals were being driven off their land, treated as inferiors and aliens. So from the first the Aboriginal felt that Government policies said one thing, but meant another.

If Aboriginals were to become part of white society, then obviously the authorities had a duty to educate them in this direction. This was clearly stated in British instructions to Governor Darling to 'promote Religion and Education among the Native Inhabitants.' Earlier than this, in 1814, Governor Macquarie had begun to set up an Educational Institution for Aboriginal children at Parramatta. This Government institution was the earliest attempt to introduce Aboriginals to 'Christian civilisation.' It ran into several difficulties. First, it meant taking Aboriginal children away from their parents, and the parents did not like this, except for a short time when it suited them because they had to seek new food sources. Secondly, at this time fierce fighting broke out in the area between whites and blacks, which must have made the Aboriginals even less desirous of having their children become like white men. Thirdly, the authorities found that Aboriginals at Parramatta were tending to adopt the white man's vices such as drink.

This was a small experiment only and was soon abandoned. On a small scale it gave a picture of what was to happen over the next 150

Do you think that these Aboriginal children would have found this sort of lesson an interesting one? The photograph was taken in Queensland probably in the 1890s.

years throughout Australia. The white man was to make attempts at educating some Aboriginals to become like white men (this is sometimes called *assimilation*). This failed because Aboriginals did not want themselves or their children to be assimilated, to become like white men. It also failed because if one or two Aboriginals did acquire the white man's learning and customs, they still found they were not fully accepted; they were not treated as equals, but as inferiors. Rusden in his *History of Australia* quotes one of these Aboriginals as saying: '. . . I cannot be a white man, they will never look on me as one of themselves; and I cannot be a blackfellow.' Such a man had been left helpless between two worlds, part of neither.

The assimilation attempts also failed because the Aboriginal, his own society having been destroyed without any new hope being offered, tended to adopt the white man's vices. This led to a growing belief among white authorities, both in Australia and England, that the Aboriginal needed 'protection' from the evils of white society. More and more the governments in Australia acted according to this belief.

If 'protection' had meant real protection from the white landtakers, or if the advance of white settlers had at least been restricted, as it was in Papua-New Guinea by the 'Restricted Areas' policy of the 1920s, this would have been good. (Under this policy, government officers went first into areas to ensure that the whites and native people got to know each other under government control, and that the whites did not destroy the local way of life.)

But 'protection' in Australia usually came (except in some areas in the centre and north) after the Aboriginals had been driven off their land. They were given a new piece of land to live on, but this had no religious significance to them, and often was poor, unsuitable land, sometimes in places where there was no hunting, and no work available. On top of this, the Aboriginals were often put into institutions where they had no say as to how their lives were to be lived. They were put under a manager whose word had to be obeyed; they were treated like children—and often had become paupers, dependent on charity.

The result was that in most cases 'protection' failed to protect. This was particularly so in the earlier years, when governments made very little effort, and left the task of protection to one or two Christian missionaries. From 1824 to 1841 a devoted missionary, Reverend L. E. Threlkeld, devoted himself to making friends with the Aboriginals in the Lake Macquarie area, New South Wales. He tried to help and protect them, and translated St Luke's Gospel into the Awabakal language. But in his annual reports he told how one tribe of 164 persons had dwindled to three in the space of four years, how large numbers were being destroyed by 'spirits', or 'force of arms', by measles, whooping cough and influenza, through convicts taking Aboriginal women by 'force, fraud or bribery', or by wholesale slaughter by mounted police combined with stockmen. Finally, in 1841, he had to report that 'The Mission to the Aborigines has ceased to exist . . . purely from the Aborigines themselves becoming extinct in these parts . . .' The Gospel exists today in the Awabakal language—but there is no one to read it.

As a comparison with the picture on page fifty-three, here are children being taught by pre-school teaching assistant Katie Bulguda at Maningrida, Northern Territory

Later, where missionaries had a respect for the Aboriginal way of life, and where the governments gave them enough land, they were able to give real protection—as at Ernabella in South Australia. But many missionaries, though well-meaning, had little understanding of, or respect for, the Aboriginal people. This prevented them from being real protectors.

Also, it was clear from the first that the Churches did not have sufficient money to be able to tackle the tasks of 'protection.' Government action was needed. But the governments did little, apart from giving some grants of land to church missions. In New South Wales it was not until 1881 that a 'Protector of Aborigines' was appointed, and his funds even then were only a few hundred pounds. An 'Aborigines

Protection Board' was set up in 1883, but it had no statutory power until 1909, and, according to an official document, 'throughout practically the whole of this period the chairmanship of the Board was in the hands of the Inspector-General of Police.' In general, the governments saw the police as the 'protectors', and since Aboriginals had learned to see the police as people who persecuted them, the 'Protection Boards' became known to the Aboriginal people as 'Persecution Boards.'

And it was true that 'protection' did express itself largely (and more and more so up until about 1930) by the attempts to *control* the Aboriginal people—to keep them in Church or Government institutions under the control of a manager, and to pass special laws which may have been meant to protect Aboriginals, but which certainly denied them equal rights.

Typical of these laws (which differed from State to State) were those forbidding the sale of alcohol to Aboriginals. The result of these laws (as with Prohibition in America) was that Aboriginals continued to get alcohol—but had to pay more money for worse liquor which was often gulped down quickly to avoid arrest, but which probably led to a prison cell anyway.

The early government policy of doing nothing, or next to nothing about education of Aboriginals was continued for a long time. In 1880, when the New South Wales Department of Education accepted responsibility for the education of children in the State, Aboriginal children were not included. Over the next fifty years most of them were 'educated' by untrained teachers (perhaps a manager on a reserve) to a level of third grade primary only. By 1939 a few of these children were reaching fourth grade primary level. Even after that, on a number of occasions Aboriginal children were excluded from state schools in some country towns because of resistance by white parents to their admission. In other words, many Aboriginal adults alive today were refused a full primary education. In most other States the position was even worse than in New South Wales.

In general, 'assimilation' failed to assimilate, and 'protection' failed to protect, and the plight of Aboriginals grew worse and worse.

Smoothing the Dying Pillow

> 'I realised that they were passing from us. I must make their passing easier.'
> —Daisy Bates, in *The Passing of the Aborigines*

In 1888, a writer in a book called *Picturesque Australasia* stated that '... the Australian native is slowly but surely passing away from off the face of the earth. Indeed, in one portion of Australasia—viz., Tasmania —the race is quite extinct. That this should be so is to some extent to be regretted.'

This viewpoint was widespread. The original Australians, it was held, were a 'dying race'—and there was no need to worry too much about it. Even those who believed that something should be done tended to suggest that all we could do was to be kind to these people in their last years, to 'smooth the dying pillow.'

Even as late as 1938, this attitude was expressed in a book which became widely read, a book by a woman who had lived many years of her life among Aboriginals. The woman was English-born Mrs Daisy Bates, who from 1899 to 1934 travelled hundreds of miles in her buggy and lived many years in small tents among the Aboriginals of Western and Central Australia, studying their way of life and trying to help them.

When she published her experiences in book form in 1938, the title she chose was *The Passing of the Aborigines*. She saw them as a dying race. All we could do was to make their passing easier. In her book she gave many reasons why Aboriginals were dying. In Broome she saw them in prison 'chained to each other by the neck.' Near Sandstone she found police arresting Aboriginals on the principle that if one black man has committed a crime, it is good enough to arrest any black man.

In the same area she saw police taking part-Aboriginal children away from their mothers. (This tearing apart of families was part of Australian government policies for a period when it was held that

Daisy Bates

Aboriginals of full descent should be 'protected' and part-Aboriginals 'assimilated'.)

Daisy Bates saw Aboriginals dying from white man's diseases; she saw the breakdown of life caused by 'change of food, environment, outlook, the burying of old traditions and customs . . .' She saw them dying inside Christian missions as they were dying outside—'the same story everywhere, a kindness that killed as surely and swiftly as cruelty would have done.'

She visited Rottnest Island, an Aboriginal prison where she saw men 'chained in gangs', forced to work by day, 'shepherded at night into the clammy cells of a low-roofed stone gaol, cells filthy and fever-ridden . . . prison rations . . . no fires . . . These unfortunates died in appalling numbers . . .'

Daisy Bates lived with Aboriginal people at various places in Western

Australia, then in South Australia. At Ooldea Siding near the Transcontinental Railway she lived for years in a tent enlarged by an upturned tank and a shed made of boughs. She attended to the illnesses of the Aboriginals, and gave them flour, tea and sugar bought with her own money.

She became known as Kabbarli to the Aboriginals; she was made a Commander of the British Empire by the Government. Her theory that the Aboriginals were a dying race was accepted by many Australians. It was an easy idea to accept, for if the Aboriginals were dying out then it didn't matter so much how one behaved to them. But was it true?

Daisy Bates lived mainly among the last remnants of tribes that had been destroyed, people with nothing left in life except to live on charity. These people were certainly dying out. Daisy Bates had helped to bury them. 'By the end of the great drought,' she wrote, 'there were nine graves in the sandhills about my tent.'

But she was wrong about Aboriginals being a dying race. By the time her book was published (1938), it had become clear that the number of Aboriginals of full descent was becoming steady. This was particularly so in the Centre and North, where large Aboriginal reserves had been declared by the Governments, giving some real protection. And throughout Australia the part-Aboriginal population was increasing at a considerable rate.

It is impossible to get exact figures. But for Aboriginals of full descent it is estimated that the number fell from about 250,000 or 300,000 in 1788 to about 40,000; by about 1940 or 1950 the decline had been halted; since then there is evidence of growth, and estimates for 1976 vary from 40,000 to 55,000. The number of Aboriginals of partial descent is increasing rapidly and has been estimated at about 40,000 in 1961 and about 70,000 in 1976.

This means that in 1976 there were about 120,000 Aboriginals—using the word in its broad sense—or nearly one per cent of all Australians, and the number is increasing. All of these are not leading the traditional Aboriginal life, but they are all Aboriginals.

Daisy Bates was wrong. The Aboriginals are here to stay. As this fact was realised in the 1930s, it led to changes in government policies. No longer could it be a question of 'protecting' the last dying remnants. Governments had to choose between *segregation* (keeping black people apart from whites, as in South Africa under apartheid) and some sort of togetherness such as assimilation.

Most people felt it was good that the governments chose assimilation rather than apartheid as official policy in statements from 1937 onwards from conferences of representatives of State and Federal Governments. But (and it is a big 'but') first of all the governments continued their 'protectionist' policy of controlling Aboriginals and refusing them equality, with the suggestion that assimilation could only take place after long years of education and by one or two persons at a time. (In some States such people were granted 'exemption certificates' which gave them equal rights; many Aboriginals hated this scheme and called the certificates 'dog licences'.)

And secondly, officials in some States understood 'assimilation' to mean absorption—that the Aboriginal future lay in disappearing into the white community, either by being separated so thoroughly that no two Aboriginal families would live together, or else by inter-breeding. The assimilation policy did have good points in that it implied togetherness and equality, but it was put into practice in such a way that many Aboriginals rejected the idea. Bert Groves, for instance, at the 1958 Aboriginal Federal Conference, said: 'What does assimilation imply? Certainly, citizenship and equal status—so far, so good; but also the disappearance of the Aboriginals as a separate cultural group, and ultimately their physical absorption by the European part of the population.' Later, he said: 'I don't like the word "assimilation" . . . The intelligent Aboriginal doesn't want to be absorbed into the white race. He wants to take his place in life, but he doesn't want to change his color to do it.'

Mr Groves and other members of the Aboriginal Advancement movement adopted the word 'integration' to express their aims—the word implying that Aboriginals are welcomed into the community on an equal basis with full rights to live in groups if they want to and to maintain and develop their own cultural and other activities if they wish to. This has been the policy for migrant groups in Australia. But for long years it was denied to the First Australians.

New Waves of Protest

> 'The New Zealanders are proud of the Maoris. We ask you to be proud of the Australian Aborigines.'
> —Statement by Aborigines Progressive Association, 26 January, 1938

Down through the years the Aboriginal people have resisted and protested. Year after year their protests were ignored. But in the 1930s there was an upsurge in the protest as two new groups of people joined in. The first group consisted of Aboriginal men and women in the southern states. The second group consisted of white people.

There had always been some small groups of white Australians who spoke up for the Aboriginals—church people and others who formed committees like the Association for the Protection of Native Races. Such people had worked hard, but had not been powerful enough to have much influence. But in the 1930s they were joined by anthropologists like Professor A. P. Elkin who had a high respect for the Aboriginal way of life, and by writers and trade union officials inspired by humanist or socialist ideals of human brotherhood. These people spoke out in 1934 when some Northern Territory Aboriginals were charged in a Darwin court after they had killed Japanese from pearling ships. An Aboriginal named Tuckiar was alleged to have killed a policeman.

Reports of the trials raised two questions—was it fair to punish Aboriginals for actions which were right by their own law but wrong by white man's law?—and was the Tuckiar trial a fair one by British law? When Tuckiar was sentenced to death, and other Aboriginals to twenty years gaol, a protest meeting was held in Sydney on 6 August, 1934, which some people see as a turning point in Aboriginal history. For the first time influential people from many sectors of society joined in a protest that led to inquiries by the British Government and that shook the authorities here. It was to be the beginning of many years of such united protest. (That the trial had in fact been unjust was indicated by the fact that an appeal to a higher court upset the original verdict, and Tuckiar was set free—only to disappear mysteriously on his long journey home.)

The united protest was important. Equally important—perhaps more important—was the fact that Aboriginal people in the southern states were organising themselves for a better deal. An 'Australian Aborigines' Progressive Association' in Sydney from about 1924 to 1927 had died out, but in the New South Wales countryside a trade unionist named William Ferguson, of Scottish and Aboriginal descent, began planning a new organisation. He found help from men like Charles Leon, John Patten, Bert Groves, Jack Kinchela, and later Bill Onus, also keen workers for their people.

The Depression of the 1930s had made things hard for white Australians, but they were even harder for Aboriginals. If unemployed whites were on the starvation level, then most Aboriginals were below it; work was even harder to get than for whites; housing and health were worse. Discrimination was practised in many country towns where Aboriginals were shunned in shops and streets and roped off in the front of picture theatres. And the controls of the Government Protection Acts refused equality.

It was amid such conditions that Bill Ferguson, on 27 June, 1937 called a public meeting at Dubbo to launch the Aborigines' Progressive Association. He was a big man, a good speaker, and from his trade union, the Australian Workers' Union, he had learnt the value of organisation, of public protest, of influencing politicians. The three main aims of the new Association were full citizen rights for Aboriginals, representation in Parliament like that of the Maoris in New Zealand, and abolition of the New South Wales Aborigines Protection Board—which was seen as an instrument of unfair control and inequality.

Ferguson soon won considerable support, and the Labor Party got a motion through State Parliament (against Government opposition) for a Select Committee Inquiry into the Aborigines Protection Board. This Inquiry dragged on for a long time and did not lead to any immediate reforms, but it had two good results. First, it gave some

Aboriginal rights leader Bill Ferguson speaking at the Sydney Domain in 1949

publicity to the plight of men and women who for a long time had been a forgotten people.

Here for instance are some statements by Mr G. N. Milne, who had worked as an assistant at Cummeragunga (Cummeroogunga) Aboriginal Station near the Murray:

'I found that the natives did not get a fair go . . . they lived on damper, or "Johnny cakes" . . . Housing conditions were appalling. Down on the banks of the river there were about a dozen bag huts with no floors . . . I have seen people lying on the floor with one blanket between them . . . There was no sympathy towards the Aboriginal. I have spoken to Aboriginals on various matters on which they are dissatisfied, and they would say: "What is the use of reporting the matter to the

Board? The letter will come back to you. No one takes the word of an Aboriginal." '

Asked: 'Their impression is that the Aboriginal is looked down upon as something inferior to the white man?' Mr Milne replied: 'Yes.'

Secondly, it brought Bill Ferguson in touch with other people who were developing as Aboriginal leaders, including two from Melbourne —William Cooper and young footballer Doug Nicholls (later to become Sir Douglas Nicholls, South Australian Governor). Ferguson was also brought closer to Jack Patten, Margaret Tucker and Pearl Gibbs, and to white Australians like Michael Sawtell, writers Xavier Herbert and P. R. Stephensen, Labor politician Mark Davidson and trade union official Tom Wright. Together these people began to prepare for a big day—26 January, 1938, the 150th anniversary of the landing of Governor Phillip.

For some months Bill Cooper had been urging that his people should make this a public 'Day of Mourning', and now plans were made for this to be centred in Sydney with an Aboriginal Conference, distribution of pamphlets, and a petition to the Prime Minister, Mr Lyons.

The pamphlet addressed white Australians in strong words: 'You are the New Australians, but we are the Old Australians. We have in our arteries the blood of the Original Australians, who have lived in this land for many thousands of years. You came here only recently, and you took our land away from us by force. You have almost exterminated our people, but there are enough of us remaining to expose the humbug of your claim, as white Australians, to be a civilised, progressive, kindly and humane nation. By your cruelty and callousness towards the Aborigines you stand condemned in the eyes of the civilised world. These are hard words, but we ask you to face the truth of our accusation.' The pamphlet went on: 'We ask for equal education, equal opportunity, equal wages, equal rights to possess property or to be our own masters—in two words: *equal citizenship*!'

Soon after this, on 4 February, 1939, Aboriginal people on Cummeraguna in a mass walkout crossed into Victoria in protest at their treatment and the arrest of Jack Patten on the reserve; they stayed out for months but were forced back by starvation.

Press cuttings of the 1950s show some of the problems faced by the Aboriginals

Bitter opposition to de-segregation

DARWIN, Monday. — White parents withdrew their children from Elliott primary school today when five full-blood aboriginal children attended.

Protest by aborigines

Many aborigines at Redfern were too frightened to walk the streets because of police victimisation, native community leaders claimed this week.

They said that during holiday periods innocent as well as guilty aborigines were "scooped from the streets" in police raids.

Bid To Give Full Poll Rights To Natives Defeated

CANBERRA, Wednesday.—The Government tonight defeated by 57 votes to 39 an Opposition move to give aborigines full voting rights in Federal elections.

CHILD DEATHS "FOR YEARS" IN WALGETT DISTRICT

From A Special Reporter

WALGETT, Wednesday. — For years undernourished aboriginal children have been dying near Walgett, the Rev. A. R. Ewin said today.

Aborigines living in shanties outside Condobolin had to use water polluted by refuse and dead animals, townspeople said this week.

Tues. — White residents of the Gippsland hamlet of Nowa Nowa are threatening to move if three aboriginal families are housed in the town.

Natives fined: on tribal ground

DARWIN, Tues.—Police arrested a group of aborigines on Sunday for being in the area where they were born, but which is now prohibited to them.

This movement by the Aboriginal people themselves had results. The New South Wales Government announced a new policy of 'welfare' to replace 'protection', and replaced the old Protection Board with the slightly more sympathetic Aborigines Welfare Board, on which the Aboriginal people of New South Wales could elect two members.

This sounded good. But to Bill Ferguson the position was still 'dreadful', for his people were still denied equality, and though he was elected to the Welfare Board, he and his fellow Aboriginal member were in a hopeless minority. Even when war came in 1939 and many Aboriginal people enlisted, the Government declared, after accepting about 3,000 in the first eighteen months, that such enlistment was to be discouraged.

There were many such setbacks. Bill Ferguson and the Aboriginal organisations struggled on, but finally, in 1949, Ferguson became convinced that Aboriginals could not depend on the politicians to do things for them. He resigned from the Labor Party (after thirty-two years membership), and stood for Federal Parliament in the seat of Lawson, in western New South Wales, as an independent. He got only 388 votes in a total of over 37,000. He died soon after, and his life may have seemed a failure. But his life story has been told in a recent book by Jack Horner, and many Aboriginal people remember him as a wise and courageous leader.

After his death there appeared to be a falling off in Aboriginal protest for a time. But public interest in Aboriginal questions was being roused by a number of events. One of these was the treatment of Fred Waters, an Aboriginal official of the North Australian Workers' Union, who in 1951 organised a strike of Darwin Aboriginals asking for better wages and food, and was arrested and deported to a distant area called Haasts Bluff, about 1,000 miles from his family and his land.

This led to such wide protests, particularly from the trade unions, that Waters was released. But there was even greater interest in another case, which deserves a separate chapter.

Albert Namatjira

> 'When he died, even the London *Times*, which is by no means uncritical in the notice it takes of white Australian citizens or extravagant in the space it devotes to Australian affairs, printed an obituary of nearly two hundred words on the Aboriginal artist. Yet Namatjira died, leaving behind him little wealth to bequeath to his family, his pride deeply humiliated by a prison sentence, a broken man, disillusioned with himself and with the people about him. Today the shadow of his failure still lies heavily on those of us who knew him and who loved him.'
> —T. G. H. Strehlow in *Nomads In No-Man's-Land*, 1960

Albert Namatjira was a Central Australian Aboriginal of the Aranda tribe born in 1902 on the Hermannsburg Lutheran Mission. In this area there were no bark paintings, and the Aboriginals were not well known as artists, but Namatjira, with tuition from white Australian artist Rex Battarbee, became such a renowned watercolorist that in 1954 he was brought to Sydney as a guest of honour at the time of the Queen's visit; sixty-four of his sixty-eight paintings exhibited sold within a few days.

But although he was honored in this way, the authorities had prevented him from buying a building block in Alice Springs or a grazing lease, and in an interview with a Sydney *Sun Herald* reporter on 28 February, 1954, he said his people were tired of 'walking around reserves like animals.' He added: 'I have painted for twenty years and always I have had to guard my paintings when the wet comes so that the rain does not soak them as it soaks me. Sometimes, when I am in a tent away from home, the rain does find them, and then my colours run and they are spoiled. This is no good. I am old now and I am tired of moving with my tent. I would like to settle before it is too late . . . There is a reserve for us in the Alice, but we do not like it . . . We would like to have a little place of our own . . . I am sad.'

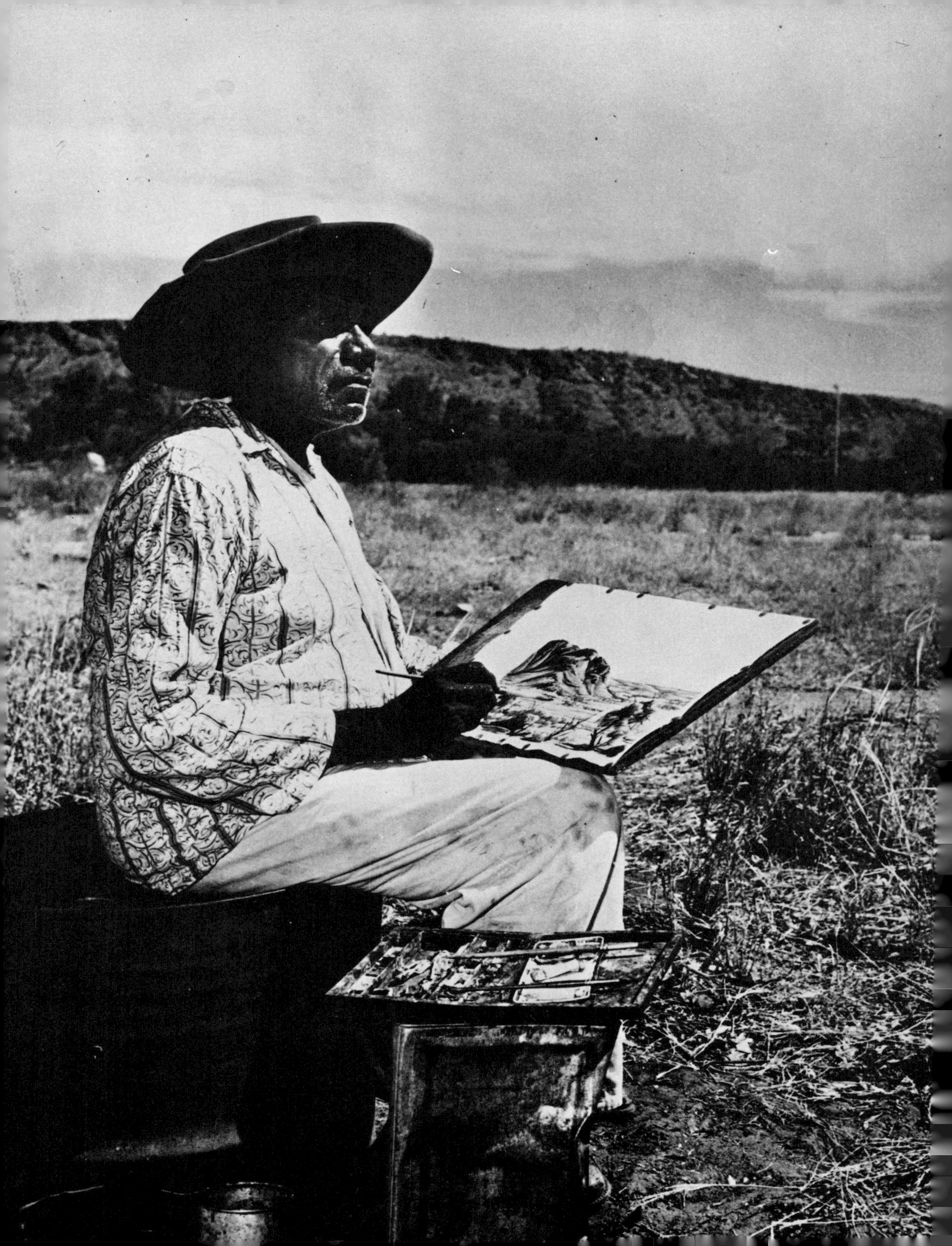

In 1954 Namatjira had been brought to court because he had sipped a little alcohol. He had been acquitted. Later he was given 'citizenship rights' which meant he could no longer be gaoled for taking a sip of alcohol. But in 1958 he was arrested and charged in Alice Springs with supplying liquor to Aboriginals. He had allegedly been drinking and had handed a bottle of rum to a tribesman, an act of sharing which was the right thing for him to do according to Aboriginal custom. But white men's law at that time prescribed a penalty for anyone giving alcohol to an Aboriginal, and although this law was originally passed to protect Aboriginals from white men, it was now used against Australia's best-known Aboriginal. Namatjira was sentenced to six months in gaol (the minimum sentence under the regulations). An appeal reduced the sentence to three months, and he was allowed to serve it on a reserve. He was released after two months, but was reported to have been very upset at the sentence, and to have said: 'Why don't they just shoot us and save all this trouble if we can't be allowed to live like men?'

Soon after his release, in August 1959, Albert Namatjira died suddenly. Writer Frank Clune commented: 'The doctors can say as much as they like about heart attacks. But I'll always believe old Albert died of a broken heart.'

These events probably caused more heart-searching among Australians as to our attitudes to Aboriginals than any other event in our history.

Their effect was strengthened by the fact that in Western Australia a group of Aboriginals, in spite of great difficulties, had organised a strike in 1945 for better wages and conditions on the big cattle stations of the Pilbara district. They had then formed a successful co-operative which showed that Aboriginals could organise better conditions for themselves than were obtainable from white men. In the 1945 strike, the Aboriginals were only demanding a thirty shilling (three dollars) weekly wage and reasonable food and housing, but their leaders were gaoled. But they set up their co-operative camp, organising hunting and fishing, and later other activities such as extracting minerals from earth, using the old Aboriginal method of 'yandying.' This had been used to

Albert Namatjira

separate grass seed grain from the husks by moving them with a special wrist movement in a bark container such as a coolamon; now it was used to separate the heavy mineral from the lighter earth. This group was written about by Donald Stuart in his novel *Yandy* and by Dorothy Hewett in her poem *Clancy and Dooley and Don McLeod*. (Three of the leaders were the two Aboriginals Clancy McKenna and Dooley, and Scots contractor Donald McLeod, who for years has lived with and advised this Aboriginal group, still in existence in 1977 near Port Hedland.)

The bad news of the death of Namatjira, and the good news of the success of the Western Australian co-operative (which had considerable help from trade unions) combined to give fresh strength to organisations working for Aboriginal Advancement. They set out to overcome what had been one of their main weaknesses—that the bodies in the different States were out of touch with each other, and had no united voice.

Federal Advancement Council

> 'This was a very historic occasion, as it is the first time that these organisations have come together to formulate a united policy and to seek to actively co-operate in the work they have been doing independently for the advancement of the Aboriginal people.'
> —Statement of the first Federal Conference, 1958

In previous chapters there has been mention of the Aborigines' Advancement League in Victoria, and the Aborigines' Progressive Association in New South Wales. There had been similar bodies in other States—all doing good work separately, but without a common voice. On 14 February, 1958 delegates from nine of these bodies from the five mainland States met together in Adelaide, and set up for the first time a 'Federal Council for Aboriginal Advancement.'

The nine bodies did not join together; each remained in existence to work in its own State, but they agreed on a common policy, and elected a Council of seven members to function as a leadership in between annual conferences—a leadership that could speak on behalf of Aboriginal Advancement organisations throughout Australia.

Seven general principles were agreed on, followed by eleven points for carrying them out. The main principles, in brief, were (1) Repeal of all legislation, Federal and State, which discriminates against Aboriginals, (2) The Commonwealth Constitution to be amended to give the Federal Government power to legislate to assist Aboriginals because of their special disabilities, (3) Improved housing, (4) Equal pay for equal work, (5) Improved education, (6) Retention of all remaining reserves, with Aboriginal communal or individual ownership, (7) Improved ration scales.

Of twelve delegates, three were Aboriginal—Pastor Doug Nicholls (Victoria), Bert Groves (New South Wales) and Jeff Barnes (South

Australia). The fact that only a minority of the delegates were Aboriginal was due to a number of reasons. Probably the main reason was that most of the Aboriginal people were living far away from the big cities; this made it difficult for them to organise except on a local scale. The treatment of Aboriginals in the past meant that there were not yet many with the education and the organising abilities of Bill Ferguson or Doug Nicholls.

It was also a factor that in the 1950s a considerable number of white Australians, as they learnt more of men like Namatjira and of the treatment of his people, wanted to join the Aboriginal protest; they were ashamed of the position and wanted to help change it. So it was natural that the advancement movement should be one of blacks and whites together.

At the second annual conference—in Melbourne in 1959—it was decided that the Council should be open not only to Aboriginal Advancement bodies, but to all organisations which subscribed to its principles. This meant that trade unions, church bodies, women's leagues and student bodies could join, and this added considerable strength to the Council, financially and also in other ways; its discussions and decisions began to win space in the newspapers. It had become a force in Australia.

Also, its existence brought the Aboriginal people closer together, and gave them confidence and experience. Further strength was gained when Torres Strait Islanders, also denied full citizenship, joined up, and the Council became the Federal Council for Advancement of Aborigines and Torres Strait Islanders (FCAATSI for short).

But the tasks faced were enormous. This was largely due to the fact that when the Australian constitution had been agreed on, the power to make laws for Aboriginals had been given to State Governments. Each State had its own laws. In one State an Aboriginal could drink alcohol; in another he could not. In one State he could own property, in another he could not. In one he could vote, in another he could not. And so on, in a complicated maze of restrictive laws.

As FCAATSI and other bodies intensified their protests, most States began to change their laws. In New South Wales, for instance, Aboriginals were given equal drinking rights, and legal equality in other ways. Every year FCAATSI could point to gains—and yet the

Mrs Geraldine Briggs from Victoria addressing a conference organised by the Aboriginal-Australian Fellowship in Sydney in 1965. Veteran leaders of their people Mrs Pearl Gibbs and Mr Alex Vesper can be seen among those listening. This was one of the first conferences at which most of the addresses were given by Aboriginals themselves.

Aboriginal people remained a depressed people, held down by problems of health, housing and unemployment far greater than those for white people.

Their position was recognised in an official Ministry of Territories booklet in 1959 which was called *Fringe Dwellers*, and which wrote of 'those native people who have already lost touch, or are losing touch, with their Aboriginal way of life and have not yet been fully received into the white Australian community . . . In varying degrees, therefore, most of these people are 'fringe dwellers'—people living merely on the fringes of Australian towns, of the larger Australian society, of the Australian economy, only on the fringes of hope and often on the fringes of despair.'

One reason for this was the continuing control by State Governments, lacking in funds, and in the will to make changes. So FCAATSI increased its drive to have the Federal Government given power to legislate for Aboriginals. The Labor Party supported this, then the Liberal and Country Parties, and at last the pressure of many years succeeded in getting a referendum in 1967 in which the people were asked to vote on whether the Federal Government should be given power to legislate for Aboriginals. (They were also asked whether Aboriginals should be included in the census population figures; previously they had been excluded.) By the greatest majority ever in any referendum, the people voted 'Yes.' The Federal Government now had responsibility for Aboriginals. It was an important decision.

But a change was taking place in the Aboriginal protest movement. In August 1969 the general meeting of the Aborigines Advancement League in Victoria (one of the biggest bodies in FCAATSI) issued a statement which said: 'The League exists for the benefit of Aboriginal people. Its Aboriginal members are in a position to tell the League what it should be and do to best serve the interests of Aboriginal people. Its non-Aboriginal members will stand back while those decisions are being made, and will work to put them in effect in collaboration with the Aboriginal members.'

Well-known Aboriginal poet Kath Walker at about the same time expressed similar ideas: 'If black Australians are to become masters of their own destiny, white Australians must recognise them as being capable of formulating their own policy of advancement. . . . Black Australians must strengthen themselves into a solid, determined, fighting unit and dictate their own terms for their own advancement. *They* must define what is best for their own advancement and then *they* can determine where white Australians can be of assistance.'

FCAATSI remained in existence, but many Aboriginal members left it to for a National Tribal Council, an all-Aboriginal body.

The 1960s had been a period in which a black and white coalition had been speaking up for Aboriginals and bringing pressure to bear on State Governments. This had ended. The 1970s were to be a period in which

Aboriginals themselves were to speak and organise and develop their own leadership, bringing their pressure to bear mainly on the Federal Government.

Some Outstanding Aboriginals

> 'Out of their treasures, old and new, the Aborigines can enrich Australian life. Whether they do so or not will depend on White Australians as much as on themselves.'
> —Professor A. P. Elkin, *The Australian Aborigines*

Very few Aboriginals have had a chance to become well-known. But some have succeeded in spite of everything.

There were many brave men among Australia's early explorers, and a number of them were Aboriginals. Again and again, white explorers succeeded when they co-operated with Aboriginals, and failed when they ignored them. Flinders praised Bungaree, who sailed with him round Australia, as 'a worthy and brave fellow.' Wylie was a worthy companion to Eyre, Yuranigh's 'courage, honesty and fidelity' were praised by Mitchell, Jacky-Jacky showed his courage with Kennedy; the Forrest brothers praised Tommy Windich for his 'intelligence and fidelity.'

Bungaree ended his days a pathetic figure in cast-off white man's clothing with a false brass plate round his neck: 'Bungaree—King of the Blacks.' And when the Eyre Highway across the Nullarbor was opened in 1976, a journalist who sought Wylie's grave discovered that it had been forgotten. He finally found it marked by nothing but a fencepost. (Aboriginals played an important role not only in the exploration of Australia, but also in the settlement of vast areas in the Centre and North by supplying the necessary labor force, but their work, like their names, tends to be forgotten.)

Aboriginals led the way in cricket too. The first Australian cricket team to tour England was an Aboriginal team, that won fourteen and drew nineteen matches of forty-seven played against top English teams in 1868. The tour is commemorated by a granite cairn at Edenhope High School, Victoria.

The first Australian cricket team to tour England was entirely composed of Aboriginals. The tour took place in 1868.

For many years Aboriginals didn't get much chance to become prominent, but in recent years they have broken through again and again. Harold Blair, born at Murgon, Queensland, in 1924, became one of our best-known singers, and when he died early in 1976 it was announced that a memorial would be built at Shepparton, Victoria, in the form of a Harold Blair Memorial Aboriginal Museum. Following Harold Blair came Captain Reg Saunders, one of Australia's best-known soldiers—in spite of the fact that Aboriginals were not supposed to join the Army!

In 1953 two Aboriginals, Robert Tudawali and Rosalie Kunoth, became widely known when they played the leading roles in Charles Chauvel's film *Jedda*. Rosalie returned to Alice Springs; later she married and was living in Melbourne. Tudawali continued as an actor and won praise for his part in the film *Dust In The Sun*, and was in Sydney for TV films in 1960. But on Christmas Day of the previous year he had been gaoled in Darwin for six months for handing an Aboriginal mate a pannikin of wine. One Sydney paper had carried the headline: 'Australia's No. 2 Black Man Gaoled—No. 1 Died Of A Broken Heart.' After 1960 there was little or no work acting, and Tudawali was reported to be looking 'gaunt and ill', and to have told friends: 'I am just another blackfellow now.' In July 1967 he died of burns in Darwin Hospital. His death was reported under the words: 'The Tragedy of Tudawali.'

Tudawali's wife was a niece of another famous Aboriginal—Mosik, described by American dancer Ted Shawn as one of the greatest dancers of the world. He was one of many fine dancers; a group of forty-five dancers from Arnhem Land was highly praised in 1963 when it toured Australia as 'Aboriginal Theatre.'

This book has already mentioned Albert Namatjira. There were a number of other artists in his group who have won fame; they include his sons Enos, Oskar and Ewald and son-in-law Claude Pannka, and others like Edwin, Otto and Reuben Pareroultja, Walter Ebaterinja, Henoch Raberaba and Richard Moketarinja. And in the North there have been famous artists like Yirawala painting on bark.

For many years Pastor Doug Nicholls was well-known as a leader of his people and a popular sportsman (an interstate Australian Rules wingman); in 1976 he had become Sir Douglas Nicholls and was designated as Governor of South Australia among congratulations from his many friends. He is one of many famous Aboriginal sportsmen, the first place going to New South Wales country girl Evonne Goolagong who became Wimbledon champion and one of the top tennis players in the world—after her marriage still playing and winning as Evonne Cawley.

There have been so many top-ranking Aboriginal boxers that it is difficult to give a full list; names that come to mind are the Sands brothers, George Bracken, Ron Richards, Jack Hassen, Elley Bennett, Lionel Rose of course, Hector Thompson—many others could be added. Other well-known sportsmen include cricketer Eddie Gilbert, soccer player Harold Williams, Eric Simms and Arthur Beetson in rugby

Sir Douglas Nicholls taking part in a 1973 re-enactment in Melbourne of John Batman's purchase of the city site from local Aboriginals in 1835. The re-enactment was aimed at reminding the non-Aboriginal community of what happened when Europeans came to Australia, of the debt owed to the Aboriginal community, and to urge the case for compensation.

league; Graham (Polly) Farmer, Barry Cable, Michael Graham, Sid Jackson and David Kantilla in Australian Rules football; Michael Ahmatt, Olympic basketballer; and Faith Thomas, Australian women's cricketer.

In recent years, a number of Aboriginal poets have come to the fore. Kath Walker from Brisbane became well-known as a leader of her people, and even better known as a poet; in 1970 she was reported to be 'the best-selling poet, apart from C. J. Dennis, in Australia's history.' Here are some of her lines in which she rejects the 'assimilation' demand that Aboriginals must become like white men:

> ...... *Do not ask of us*
> *To be deserters, to disown our mother,*
> *To change the unchangeable.*
> *The gum cannot be changed into an oak.*
> *Something is gone, something surrendered, still*
> *We will go forward and learn.*
> *Not swamped and lost, watered away, but keeping*
> *Our own identity, our pride of race.* .....

Jack Davis from Western Australia, also a leader of his people and a fighter for their rights, at times expresses in his poems his anger with the white man: 'You have turned our land into a desolate place.' But in poems like *Integration* he sees a future in which black and white can learn from each other and live together:

> *It is time to learn.*
> *Let us forget the hurt,*
> *Join hands and reach*
> *With hearts that yearn.* .....

In recent years, so many Aboriginals have become prominent in a wide range of activities that it is impossible to name them all. There are many writers and artists like Dick Roughsey, Kevin Gilbert, Colin Johnson and Ronald E. Bull. There are singers like Jimmy Little. Two who indicate new directions are Charles Perkins and Senator Neville Bonner. Born at Alice Springs, Charles Perkins became well-known as a soccer player, and again as a Sydney University student when he led a 'Freedom Ride' in a bus through New South Wales towns to protest at discrimination. He is also known as author of the book *A Bastard Like Me*, and assistant secretary of the Department of Aboriginal Affairs. Neville Bonner since being elected as Liberal-Country Party senator for Queensland has represented his State—and his people—in Federal Parliament for some years.

Enough names have been given to show the ability of Aboriginals to reach the highest positions. But does the list show all is well? Or does it show how hard it was to reach the top, and how hard it has been for many Aboriginals even when they reached the top? And how much Australia might benefit if there were equal opportunity for all Australians to develop their abilities?

Part Three — ABORIGINALS TODAY

A Multi–Racial Society

> 'After two centuries of dislocation and misunderstanding, it is no simple matter for the majority community and the Aboriginal minority to enter into a partnership of mutual respect.'
> —From a Department of Aboriginal Affairs leaflet, 1974

The main fact about Australian Aboriginals today is that they are by no means a 'dying race', that they are here to stay, that their numbers are growing, and that much more than ever before they are demanding their rights, and calling for equality of opportunity.

For years many white men have acted as though Australia is inhabited only by white-skinned, English-speaking people. This never has been true, and it is much less true today than it was thirty years ago. Australia is a multi-racial and multi-cultural society—a country in which there are many different groups with different cultural backgrounds—English, Irish, Scots, Welsh, German, Chinese, Italian, Greek, Pacific Islanders, Maltese, Aboriginal and many others. We can either fight among ourselves, or we can live in friendship and learn from each other.

This is not easy. For nearly 200 years the Aboriginal people have been treated in such a way that they have become a disadvantaged people. Because they have been denied the advantages and opportunities of other people, they have fallen behind in general living standards, in housing, in health, in education, and in employment.

Since 1967, when the Federal Government was given power to deal with these matters—and particularly since 1972, when the Labor Government launched large-scale programmes for Aboriginal welfare—there has been a real attempt to tackle these problems. We will look at some of these programmes in a later chapter. But the first point to note is that however good they are, welfare programmes cannot solve problems quickly. One reason for this is that problems of a disadvantaged group tend to become mixed up with one another, to form a 'vicious circle.' Problem A is bad in itself, but it also causes Problem B, which causes Problem C, which causes Problem D, which causes Problem A, which—and so it goes on.

For instance, many Aboriginals live in areas where employment opportunities are poor. This has led to lack of money, which has led to poor housing, which has led to poor health. Poor housing and health (plus perhaps the need to move around for work) have led to poor education, which can lead to lack of employment, and so the circle goes on. In recent years, authorities have taken a number of steps to help Aboriginal children with their education, but often children have been handicapped by a variety of problems. In addition, many Aboriginal families, with some reason, looked on education as a process that fits an Aboriginal child for a job in white society and then says: 'Sorry; there is no job available.'

Problems like this are not solved easily. Each problem seems to be intertwined with other problems. And the problems are different for each State, for each area of each State, and perhaps also for each group of people in each area of each State.

Let us look now at some of the details. The 1971 census gave figures for the Aboriginal population—this includes Aboriginals of full descent and those people of mixed descent who consider themselves to be Aboriginal. The figures for the different States (not including Torres Strait Islanders) were: Australian Capital Territory 248, Tasmania 575, Victoria 5,656, South Australia 7,140, Western Australia 21,903, New South Wales 23,101, Northern Territory 23,253, Queensland 24,414.

One of the big changes has been a movement from country to town. In the past most Aboriginals lived in the country. It is difficult to get exact figures of the percentage living in towns, but the census figures, such as they are, show that in 1961 about 23 percent of Aboriginal people lived in towns of over 1,000 inhabitants; in 1966 about 27 per cent; and in 1971 about $43\frac{1}{2}$ per cent.

This is still much less than for the total Australian population, of whom over 80 per cent are urban; but it shows a major change. The movement has obviously taken place because so many Aboriginals have found themselves in country areas where it is impossible to find work. There are also other reasons. Some have moved to the city to get medical

The type of city living that Aboriginals have had to contend with. This was the scene before work began on the Redfern Aboriginal Housing project in Sydney. The Australian Government allocated $500,000 to the local community for the purchase and renovation of these dilapidated terrace houses in the inner city area.

treatment; others because they have found less discrimination in the big cities.

Fay Gale, whose book *Urban Aborigines* (1972) is based on a study of Aboriginal communities in Adelaide, states that the majority of Aboriginals in the city are 'better housed, better educated, better employed, in better health' than those in the country, and that the city appears to offer them 'the kind of economic and social environment in which they can achieve self-sufficiency and equality, on their terms, for perhaps the first time since European colonisation.'

There are two problems involved. One is that Aboriginals in making this change to the city, need the support and help of Aboriginal organisations. We will look at this in a later chapter. The other problem

—and a very serious one—is that in the city, as in the country, it may still be difficult, or impossible, to get good housing, and to get work. This of course is particularly so in a time of economic depression.

Generally Aboriginals in a big city have to live in areas of poor housing like Sydney's Redfern, usually with serious over-crowding as kinsfolk come from country areas seeking work. This can perhaps be overcome in periods of full employment, but the situation has been serious in times of economic depression. Journalist Neil Mitchell in the Melbourne *Age* of 30 August, 1976 reported that 'more than half of Melbourne's 4000 Aboriginals are out of work. . . . Children are suffering from severe malnutrition.' Aboriginal people said they had been refused jobs and accommodation because they were black. Children had had to face prejudice at school; a 16-year-old girl had tried to peel off her black skin and needed treatment.

The unemployment problem is obviously a major one for Aboriginals in both city and country. A Department of Aboriginal Affairs report in May 1976 estimated that more than half the Aboriginal work force for the whole of Australia was unemployed, compared with a general level of 4.4 per cent. According to a statement issued by the Aboriginal Congress in August 1976, 50 per cent of employable Aboriginal men in the Northern Territory were unemployed, and the average weekly income had fallen to between six and eight dollars. Only 5 to 10 per cent of Aboriginals in the Territory were housed, and many of these were living in sub-standard housing. There were similar reports of poor housing from all over Australia. This report from the *Sydney Morning Herald* of 24 July, 1976 is typical:

'Aboriginals in Coonamble, northern New South Wales, plan to send a delegation to Canberra to try to bring Federal Government attention to what they describe as "horrific" housing conditions. They say about 300 Aboriginals—half the community—are living in condemned houses and in overcrowded slum conditions. Their complaints are being backed up by Government officers in the area.'

That that is not unusual is indicated by the 1971 census figures for Aboriginal-occupied private dwellings. These showed that of 8,751 such rural dwellings, 3,586 or over 40 per cent were improvised dwellings. If urban dwellings are included as well as rural, the percentage of improvised dwellings is twenty-six, the percentage without gas or

Family campsites, thirty miles from Maningrida, Northern Territory

electricity is thirty, and the percentage without kitchen or bathroom is nineteen-and-a-half.

Unemployment and poor housing are of course accompanied by poor health. The Aboriginal Congress report already mentioned also quoted Dr Trevor Cutter as saying that 70 per cent of the Northern Territory's Aboriginal children suffered from chronic chest infections, 60 per cent from chronic ear infections, and 60 per cent from chronic eye infections.

In the less settled parts of Australia, large numbers of Aboriginals live on church or government settlements. In most of these in the past they have been under the control of a manager and have had little or no say. That this has been changed following Labor policies in 1972 was shown when Bill Peach in a TV feature on Arnhem Land said: 'Whites who want to move about now have to get permission from Aboriginals —that's quite a switch.' But the legacy of the past—unemployment, poor health and housing, apathy—is not changed easily. Much more money is being spent by governments, and it is easier for Aboriginals to get social welfare payments, but this has led to fresh problems. In some areas, according to an October 1976 report by a Parliamentary Committee, alcoholism has been increasing and has become a serious danger.

The different settlements differ greatly from one another. Journalist Mungo MacCallum after a mid-1976 tour of the North reported in the newspaper *Nation Review* that the settlement at Borroloola was one of the most depressing sights in the world, but that Yirrkala further north is 'everything the Borroloola is not . . . a remarkable success story.'

Economic factors have tended to work against Aboriginals in the less settled areas. Over many years the cattle industry has relied largely on the cheap labor of highly skilled Aboriginal stockmen. Recent struggles have won higher wages and better conditions for these men, but modernisation of the industry and other factors have meant that there has been less employment.

One could go on writing for ever about the position of Aboriginals today. The situation is complex, and is different everywhere. One important point is that although in general the laws which denied equality to Aboriginals have been ended, there still is discrimination. One reason for this is that while the other States have repealed discriminatory laws and have agreed to the Federal Government playing the main role, Queensland has refused to do this. It still has an Act which enables the Government through its officers and police to control the lives of all Aboriginals except those declared exempt. Large numbers live on reserves under control of a manager; conditions on Palm Island reserve in particular have come under criticism.

But apart from this, Aboriginals anywhere in Australia can be discriminated against in a number of ways—not by Acts of Parliament but by the behaviour of people. There may be no legal discrimination, but there can be social discrimination. In July 1976 a report released by the Federal Commissioner for Community Relations, Mr Grassby, stated that Aboriginals in northern New South Wales and Queensland were being discriminated against in 'education of their children, housing, employment, social community development, in business, and in lack of consultation in matters concerning their own affairs. . . . The Aboriginal communities are oppressed communities and consequently are depressed and deprived communities.'

Legally an Aboriginal may have equal rights to a job—but the employer may say no. Legally he and his family may have equal rights to accommodation—but it may be refused. Some other reason may be given—but it is still discrimination.

Mr Grassby's report stated that most whites in the areas studied held racist views towards Aboriginals, although without malice and without realising they were racist.

Aboriginal stockmen in the Northern Territory

In many areas Aboriginals claim that one of the worst forms of discrimination lies in the attitudes and actions of the police. They say that a white man can have a few drinks too many and nothing happens to him, but if an Aboriginal has a few drinks he is gaoled. Aboriginal Senator Neville Bonner has claimed that his people are 'the most incarcerated people in the world'—not because they are wicked but because of police attitudes. Aboriginal legal services established in recent years have done something to overcome this—but much remains to be done.

In South Australia some years ago an Act was passed making it a crime to discriminate racially. The Federal Government passed such an Act in 1975, and in 1977 the New South Wales Government was trying to get such an Act passed. It is generally held that such Acts can be important in checking discrimination, but that of course such Acts alone are not sufficient to end discrimination.

Finally, there are deep problems for Aboriginals even where there is no discrimination. This is particularly so in areas where the traditional way of life still largely exists, but with much influence from white society. Which life style to choose? And how does this need to be adapted to the influences from white society? And what form of education to choose—traditional Aboriginal education, or white education, or a mixture of the two, and if so what mixture? These are a few only of the many problems facing Aboriginals in the world of today.

Land Rights

> 'When Aboriginals talk about land, they're not just talking about a piece of dirt, they're talking about life.'
> —Aboriginal speaker at Land Rights discussion on Monday Conference, ABC television, September 1976

In recent years, the Aboriginal demand for land rights has more and more come to the forefront. This can mean a number of different things.

It can mean giving back to Aboriginals the whole of Australia, or a large sum of money in compensation. It can mean that a group of Aboriginals wants a permanent right to the land they are now living on. Some groups were told eighty or ninety years ago that a piece of land 'had been given to them by Queen Victoria', but they found out later that the land in fact belonged to the State Government, which at any time could decide to use the land for some other purpose—so that the group could suddenly be shifted.

Land rights can also mean that an Aboriginal group wants ownership of more than the land they are living on—they want ownership of their traditional land area, or at least a considerable part of it, including the sacred areas. Or again, land rights can mean that an Aboriginal group wants an area which is not their traditional land, but which is suitable for a cattle station or a similar enterprise, and which the group will accept in place of their traditional land.

Two major disputes in the 1960s brought the issue of Land Rights before the public eye. The first occurred in 1963 at Yirrkala, Northern Territory, where Aboriginals took a strong stand against companies wanting to mine bauxite for aluminium production. There had previously been protests when the big aluminium company Comalco had been given land from the Aboriginal reserve at Weipa in Northern Queensland. The Yirrkala Aboriginals, whose stand was supported by the superintendent of the local Methodist Mission, sent a petition written

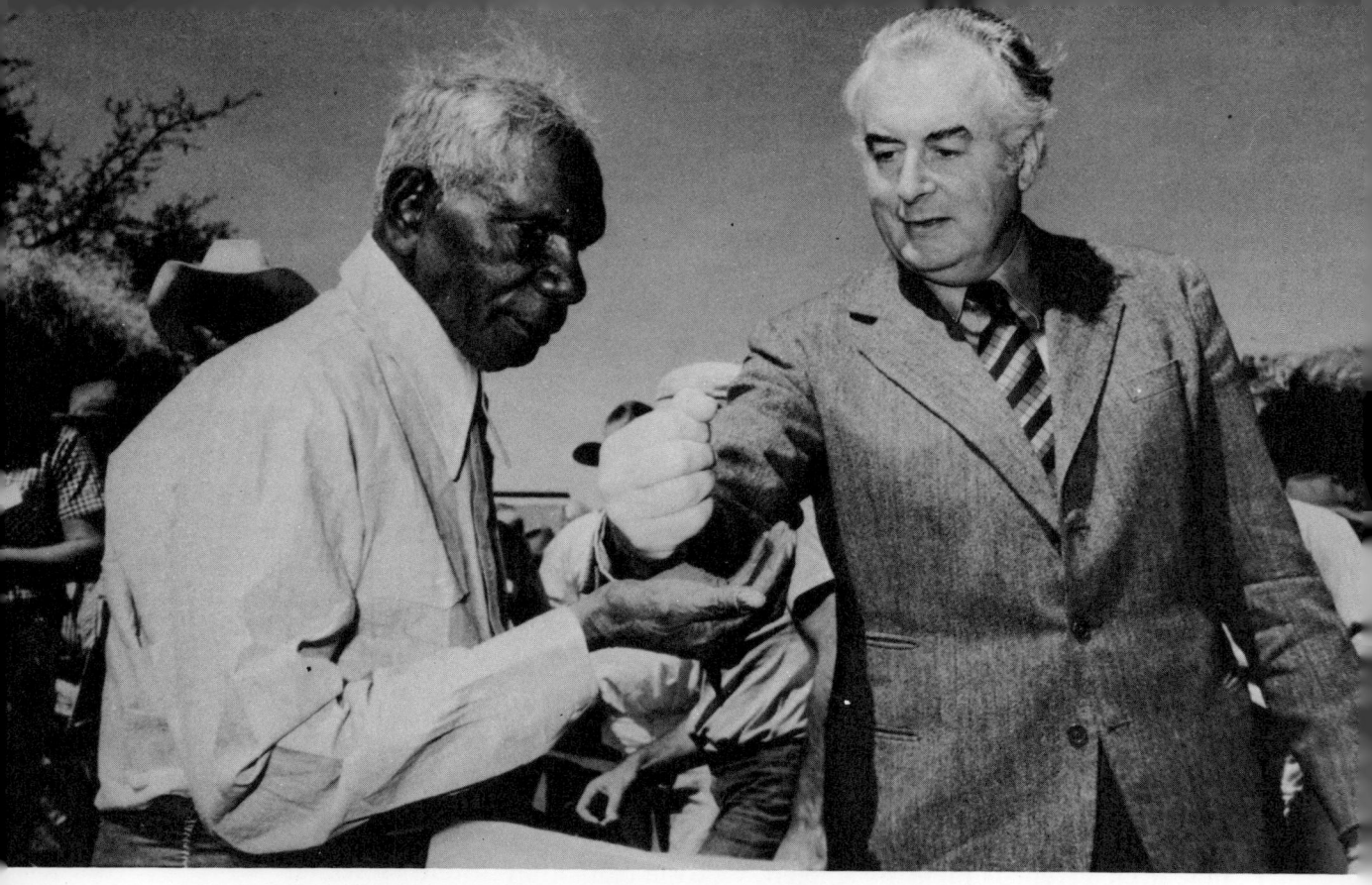

Gough Whitlam (then Australian Prime Minister) takes part in a land rights ceremony in the early 1970s

on bark to Federal Parliament. This was supported by the Labor Party and was given wide publicity. It led to the setting up of a Parliamentary Select Committee to discuss the Yirrkala situation. Eventually mining was allowed at Yirrkala only under strict conditions in line with the wishes of the Yirrkala people.

Soon after this, in August 1966, a group of about 200 Gurindjis walked off from the big Wave Hill cattle station leased by the British meat firm Vesteys in the Northern Territory. Aboriginal stockmen had for some time been calling for better wages and conditions; this time their main demand was for land. They settled on an area of their tribal land (part of the Vestey lease) at Wattie Creek, where with trade union and other support they began to build homes and get food and organise life co-operatively. They applied for a lease of 500 square miles for a cattle station of their own. It was refused. But the Gurindjis stood firm, and won wide publicity.

The coming to power of a Labor Government in December 1972 was also important for land rights. The Minister for Aboriginal Affairs, Mr Gordon Bryant (a leading member of FCAATSI over many years) announced the intention to grant a considerable area of land to the Gurindjis, and a ban on mining in Aboriginal reserves unless Aboriginals approved.

An important step was the setting up of an Aboriginal Land Rights Commission under Mr Justice Woodward. Its recommendations, accepted in principle by the Government in 1974, did not grant all the Aboriginal land claims in detail, but did establish the Aboriginal right to land in general. While this applied only to the Northern Territory, it obviously would be seen as setting a precedent for the rest of Australia. Included in the recommendations were that reserves and mission land should be handed over to full Aboriginal ownership through Land Trusts and smaller Land Councils chosen by Aboriginals, that there be no new mining on these lands unless allowed by Aboriginals (or by the Government if there is a special national interest), that Aboriginals must be always fully consulted and given as much independence as possible, that advice and funds be provided for use of the land in any sensible way Aboriginals wish, that there must be accountability by Aboriginals for use of land, resources and public money, and that steps be taken so that Aboriginals in towns have land, and also those in areas where there are no reserves.

Legislation to give effect to these important proposals was introduced on 5 November, 1975. But a few days later the Government was replaced, and the new Government proceeded to make changes, introducing the new legislation—the Aboriginal Land Rights (Northern Territory) Bill—in mid-1976. This led to considerable discussion.

Some of the discussion (still continuing as this book was being written) was about the Bill itself. The Quaker Race Relations Committee on 8 October 1976 wrote to the Prime Minister, Mr Fraser, expressing concern at the fact that 'the current Bill removes many of the safeguards to Aboriginal interests guaranteed by the 1975 Bill.' The Committee recommended that the Bill be changed to suit the wishes of the Aboriginal delegates to the Land Rights Conference held in Sydney in August 1976. Some changes were announced in November 1976.

One of the main points here is that of mineral rights. Suppose a rich mineral deposit is found under Aboriginal land (as has already happened many times). Have the Aboriginals the right to the minerals? And if not, can they refuse to allow mining if they so wish? Or allow it only on certain terms?

As the Bill stood at the end of 1976, Aboriginal groups will have a right to prohibit mining or mineral exploration on their land, but this can be overruled by the Government. But if this happens, either House of Parliament will have the right to disallow the Government's decision.

Early in 1977, newspapers reported strong difference of opinion on land rights policies between the Federal Government and the Opposition, and also between the Federal and Queensland Governments. There were also differences in a number of areas between Aboriginals and non-Aboriginals claiming the same land. The issue is clearly a complex one, and a very live one. It is likely to be particularly so in the bauxite-mining areas in the west of Cape York, where there is already a big project at Weipa, a long-continuing dispute at Mapoon, and a more recent dispute at Aurukun.

At Mapoon, Aboriginal inhabitants of a Presbyterian mission were taken away in 1963, but some have since returned. At Aurukun, there were protests at the end of 1975 when the Queensland Government put through a bill allowing large-scale mining. One of the Aboriginal elders, Albert Chevathen, said: 'We are trying to save this land for our children to help them stand firm and strong.'

The mining of uranium is also an issue on which many Aboriginal people have strong feelings. The Ranger Uranium Environmental Inquiry conducted by Mr Justice Fox in its May 1977 report referred to Aboriginal opposition to uranium mining in the Northern Territory. The report stated that the development of such mining can constitute a threat to the welfare, well-being and culture of the Aboriginal people.

The extent to which land rights will be a major issue in more settled areas is not clear. One of the main happenings in recent years has been the setting up in South Australia and New South Wales of Aboriginal Land Trusts, consisting of Aboriginal members, to hold the lands on which Aboriginal reserves are situated.

Commonwealth Programmes

'... One thing which we have learned over the last few decades is that imposed programmes, either in institutions or outside them and irrespective of how laudable the intentions may be, are self-defeating.'
—Professor C. D. Rowley in *Outcasts In White Australia*, 1970

The 1967 Referendum gave the Commonwealth Government power to legislate for Aboriginals. But the State Governments retained their power to do so, so it was possible for the Federal Government to sit back and leave most of the action to the States. At first this happened to some extent. An Office of Aboriginal Affairs was formed, and other steps taken to show that the Federal Government was now acting in Aboriginal matters. But some Aboriginals felt that not enough was being done. On 26 January, 1972 they erected tents on the lawns in front of Parliament House in Canberra, and put up a notice 'Aboriginal Embassy', with a green, black and red Aboriginal flag.

Other notices on the tents said 'Aboriginal Land Rights', and this was the main theme of the Embassy's five-point plan: (1) Control of the Northern Territory as a State within the Commonwealth of Australia; the parliament in the NT to be predominantly Aboriginal with title and mining rights to all land within the Territory. (2) Legal title and mining rights to all other presently existing reserve lands and settlements throughout Australia. (3) The preservation of all sacred sites throughout Australia. (4) Legal title and mining rights to areas in and around all Australian capital cities. (5) Compensation monies for lands not returnable to take the form of a down-payment of six billion dollars and an annual percentage of the gross national income.

Aboriginals and their friends manned the tent night and day, gave press interviews, and held an important interview with the Labor Party leader Mr Whitlam. Mr Whitlam did not agree with all the claims, but promised a Labor Government would give Aboriginal groups the ownership of reserve lands, and would protect all sacred areas. It would also ensure 'a properly representative body in the Northern Territory with full legislative powers.' (In some areas of the Northern Territory Aboriginals are in a majority.)

The Federal Government used police to demolish the embassy. But it had had an effect on public opinion, both here and overseas, and also on the December 1972 Federal elections.

For these elections, the Labor Party promised that the Office of Aboriginal Affairs would be upgraded to become a Department under a Ministry, and that this Ministry would 'work closely with Aboriginal representatives. . . . We want to know their priorities . . . not impose ours . . . a genuine plan to restore to Aboriginals their full rights as Australians.'

Labor won the election. The new Minister for Aboriginal Affairs, Mr Gordon Bryant, announced that mining would no longer be allowed on Aboriginal reserves unless the Aboriginal inhabitants approved. A number of other steps were taken to assist Aboriginal groups, the Woodward Commission on Land Rights was set up, and in 1973 Mr Whitlam announced that the Federal Government intended to take full responsibility in Aboriginal affairs. (Most States agreed to this, but not Queensland.)

In 1974, following the Woodward Commission's report, an Aboriginal Land Fund was formed with a Commission empowered to grant land or funds to Aboriginal groups, and regional Land Councils were established in some areas. A number of bodies were formed such as the Aboriginal Loans Commission and Aboriginal Sports Foundation.

A National Aboriginal Consultative Committee (NACC) was also formed. Established to advise the Minister for Aboriginal Affairs, this body is composed of more than forty Aboriginals and Islanders elected by Aboriginals and Islanders all over Australia. At the first elections in 1973 (the first nationwide Aboriginal elections ever conducted), over 28,000 people voted for the 193 candidates who stood for the forty-one electorates, the number voting being more than 80 per cent of those on the rolls.

(In May 1977 the Federal Government announced that the NACC would be replaced by a thirty-five-member National Aboriginal Con-

Mrs Faith Bandler

ference, to be elected by Aboriginals every three years. This will elect an executive which will elect five members to a Council of Aboriginal Development, five other members being appointed to this body by the Minister for Aboriginal Affairs. The Council of Aboriginal Development will replace the NACC as the chief advisory body to the Government.)

The Labor Government also greatly increased the amount of money spent on Aboriginal welfare, and it was made easier for Aboriginals to get social welfare benefits such as unemployment relief.

There have been differing viewpoints on the results of these Federal programmes. Most people have agreed that in some areas, expert advice and increased funding have resulted in successful Aboriginal enterprises. There is also general agreement that in some other areas the enterprises have not been successful. Supporters of the programmes say that some failures were inevitable, that Aboriginal groups are learning from their mistakes and that this is an essential part of developing Aboriginal initiative—letting Aboriginals learn from their own mistakes rather than letting other people make mistakes for them.

But there are other criticisms of the programmes. One is that the money spent on Aboriginal programmes is in some areas being spent in such a way that Aboriginals feel they are better off unemployed than they would be working. Thus the money spent, instead of developing Aboriginal initiative, tends to have the opposite effect, leading to idleness which tends to encourage increased alcoholism. Where this has happened, there has often been what is called a 'white backlash.' This consists in complaints from white people that too much money is being spent on Aboriginals. Such complaints can range from carefully considered opinions that money is not being spent in the best way, to obviously biased statements from people who do not understand the problems involved or who have a prejudiced viewpoint. When a retired clergyman in a New South Wales country area wrote to a newspaper complaining that Aboriginals in his area 'have become a super-privileged class', another minister in the same area replied: 'The matter is complex. It is too easy to blame the victims of a situation, thus exonerating ourselves, rather than looking at the real causes, which in this case have been going on for nearly 200 years. . . . There is a white problem as well as an Aboriginal problem.'

A further weakness of the 1972 Federal programmes was pointed out by Mrs Faith Bandler, then general secretary of FCAATSI, after a tour of Aboriginal centres. She said that Aboriginal and Island affairs were too much centralised in Canberra, that the administrators needed to be in close touch with the Aboriginal and Island people. Other people claimed that too much of the money being spent was going to white civil servants and consultants. Supporters of the Federal programmes say that these weaknesses are already being overcome, and that whatever initial mistakes were made, the 1972 Federal programmes were a major

Compare this new Northern Territory Aboriginal housing project with the pictures on page eighty-five.

step forward, ending for ever the days when Aboriginal policies were a minor matter. Now they are important, and any weaknesses will be in the limelight, and can be eliminated.

The Labor Party's 1972 policy has been quoted in part. It also includes: equal education with special programmes where needed, all Aboriginal families to be properly housed in ten years, Aboriginals to benefit from development of minerals on their lands, health to be lifted to at least the general level—and every Australian child to be taught the history and culture of Aboriginal and Island Australians as an integral part of the history of Australia.

The Liberal-National Country Party policy (1975) included: the right of Aboriginals to retain their racial identity and traditional life-style or if desired to adopt a European life-style; funding of programmes to develop Aboriginal self-sufficiency; Aboriginals to play a significant role in setting goals and priorities and formulating new programmes; Aboriginal owners to gain inalienable title to their lands and the right to determine how their lands are to be used; maintenance and expansion of Aboriginal-managed enterprises and services such as medical and legal services, Aboriginal housing, building and pastoral projects.

Most people would agree that both parties have policies which show big advances on the policies (or lack of policies) of thirty or forty years ago. But of course what actually happens in the future will depend not only on party policies, but also on political and economic pressures which may come from many directions.

New Aboriginal Bodies

> 'As I see it, the solution lies in creating an environment in which the Aboriginal can deal meaningfully with the problems he is facing (personally and as a community) ... In very broad terms, this means giving back to the Aboriginal the authority to deal with his own problems.'
> —Reverend P. G. Albrecht of the Finke River Mission

In 1946, you might have looked everywhere for an Aboriginal organisation and not found one. In 1956 you might have found one or two protest bodies. But in 1976, if you had gone to a place like the Sydney suburb of Redfern, you would have found the Aboriginal Medical Service, the Aboriginal Legal Service, the Aboriginal Black Theatre and Arts Centre, the Murawina child care centre, and a big Aboriginal housing project. These are a few only of a number of bodies which have grown up in the 1970s which are not only run *for* the Aboriginal people, but to a large extent are run *by* Aboriginal people. There are hundreds of such bodies all over Australia.

Some people, when they see Aboriginals forming their own organisations like this, may ask the question: 'Isn't this segregation? Isn't this a step backward?'

The answer is no. Segregation occurs when a particular group is forced to do things separately. If all Scottish people were forced to live in certain suburbs, or to sit in a roped-off part of theatres, that would be segregation. But if in any part of the world, Scottish people like to form a Scottish Social Club, or a Scots Association, or a Scottish Pipe Band, then that is not segregation; it is a natural activity of people with a common background and common culture who are proud of their culture and seek to preserve it.

With Aboriginals there is a special need for Aboriginal organisations. Aboriginals have for long been an oppressed people, and many of them, particularly from isolated country areas, find it very difficult to approach white people for help or advice. They need help and advice from their own people. Aboriginal organisations can also help to restore the pride of Aboriginal people in their own race and culture. (The American slogan 'Black is beautiful' is popular in Australia too.) And in Aboriginal organisations, whether they are sports bodies or welfare groups, Aboriginals can learn how to do many things, they can make mistakes and learn how to learn from their mistakes, and they can develop their own leaders. So through their own organisations, Aboriginal people can feel stronger, and can meet white people on more equal terms—giving a better basis for friendship.

When the author visited the Aboriginal Medical Service in November 1976, he was impressed by the friendly atmosphere. He talked first with the Aboriginal receptionist, Beverly Briggs, then with non-Aboriginal nursing supervisor Bill Miller. Bill said he had found it a great experience working there. 'Everyone works on an even footing, and everyone is known by his or her first name. The people you meet are sensitive, shy—but when they accept you as a friend they're friends for life.' The board of directors and nearly all the staff are Aboriginal, and it is hoped that in time there will be Aboriginal doctors.

The Service was established in 1971 thanks to the initiative of Professor F. C. Hollows and Aboriginal enthusiasts Mrs Shirley Smith, known as 'Mum Shirl' to her friends, and Mr Gordon Briscoe. After a year it was able to report that 2,000 Aboriginal patients from many areas of Sydney had received free treatment from thirty-five doctors. In November 1976 secretary-organiser Mrs. Naomi Mayers was supervising a move into new headquarters at the old St Vincent's School, with expansion to include a dental project and diabetic clinic. The Service had raised $69,000 towards the cost of the move but needed altogether $200,000—and had to date got only $50,000 from the Government, though the previous Government had promised $205,000. It wanted still more to finance other necessary expansion including regular country trips to areas where help is badly needed. There are similar Medical Services in other big cities—all needing more Government support.

Redfern Aboriginal Medical Centre, Sydney

ABORIGINAL
MEDICAL SERVICE
HOURS
MON-FRI MORNINGS
AFTERNOONS
EVENINGS
AFTER HOURS
URGENT CALLS
ABORIGINAL
MEDICAL
CENTRE

A display of artifacts made by local Aboriginals at the Yirrkala Community Store, Arnhem Land, Northern Territory. In 1971 a company was established by the Australian Government for the sale of good quality work by Aboriginal artists.

Infant mortality rates and other health statistics show that Aboriginals are severely disadvantaged in health matters, and Dr A. Kalokerinos in his book *Every Second Child* has pointed out that Aboriginal health problems differ from those of other communities and need a different approach. He adds that 'the study of Aboriginal health problems is certain to benefit people from all over the world.'

Visits to other Aboriginal organisations gave the same impression of people doing valuable work but needing more support. As this chapter was being written late in 1976, newspapers told of a fund being launched, with a target of $150,000, to save the Aboriginal Black Theatre at Redfern, which had won good reviews for its work over several years in presenting (in the words of administrator Lester Bostock) 'a theatre coming from the Aboriginal people, based on what is generally termed European theatre yet with their own particular style.'

There are so many Aboriginal bodies that it is impossible to list them all. They range from official bodies like the Aboriginal Arts Board and the New South Wales Aborigines' Advisory Council to local voluntary bodies like Tranby and Moongalba. The Aboriginal Arts Board was appointed in 1973; it is an all-Aboriginal board with artist-author Mr Dick Roughsey of Mornington Island as chairman. Its aims are preservation and revival of Aboriginal culture, and encouragement of pride in Aboriginal culture and a greater knowledge of the wide range of Aboriginal arts and crafts. The Board has had such a wide range of activities that it is impossible to summarise them, but among its many achievements have been the organising of exhibitions at home and abroad, the holding of seminars, steps towards establishing a Museum of Aboriginal Australia at Canberra and securing proper copyright for Aboriginal art forms, and encouragement of Aboriginal educational projects, literature, art, theatre and dancing. The Board's activities are part of those of the Australia Council.

The New South Wales Aborigines' Advisory Council is an official body whose nine Aboriginal members are elected by people of Aboriginal descent. Its members also constitute the Aboriginal Lands Trust for New South Wales.

Tranby, one of the older Aboriginal bodies, is a Co-Operative College at Glebe (Sydney) which since 1957 under the leadership of Reverend Alf Clint has been giving both technical skills and co-operative ideals to Aboriginal and Island people from various parts of Australia, under the official name of Co-Operative for Aborigines Ltd.—with support from trade unions, co-operatives and churches.

Moongalba is in Queensland. It has been described as 'an "alternative living" centre that gives black and white children an understanding of the Aboriginal past when life was lived with nature, rather than in opposition to it.' It was founded on Stradbroke Island by Aboriginal poet Kath Walker, as a centre where her people can come together to regain strength and pride in their race and their culture—and where white children too could learn of the Aboriginal way of life. It is a holiday place, too, a place for relaxing, getting together, for dance and theatre—a creative place.

Like many other Aboriginal centres, it lacks funds.

A number of bodies, official, semi-official and unofficial, are trying to tackle the many problems in the important field of Aboriginal education. These include local voluntary bodies assisting with pre-school education or provision of homework centres, and special university courses. As this book was being completed, a small ceremony at Sydney University marked the completion of a course of training for thirty-eight Aboriginal teaching assistants. The course director, Mr Alan Duncan, said it had been shown that such assistants made a very significant difference at schools with Aboriginal children, helping the children and establishing liaison with the Aboriginal parents. Some of them were training to become fully professional teachers.

There are scores of other Aboriginal bodies. They range from the Aboriginal Embassy still in existence in Canberra (having been given a house in exclusive Mugga Way) and bodies like Kirinari which provide hostels for Aboriginal children, to Aboriginal religious bodies and a joint Commonwealth-State scheme in New South Wales to train Aboriginals for employment, along the lines of a successful Maori scheme in New Zealand.

There are many more. In the words of Senator Neville Bonner, Aboriginals are now a force to be reckoned with.

Scene from the National Black Theatre's production of the revue *Basically Black*, performed at the Nimrod Theatre, Sydney in 1972

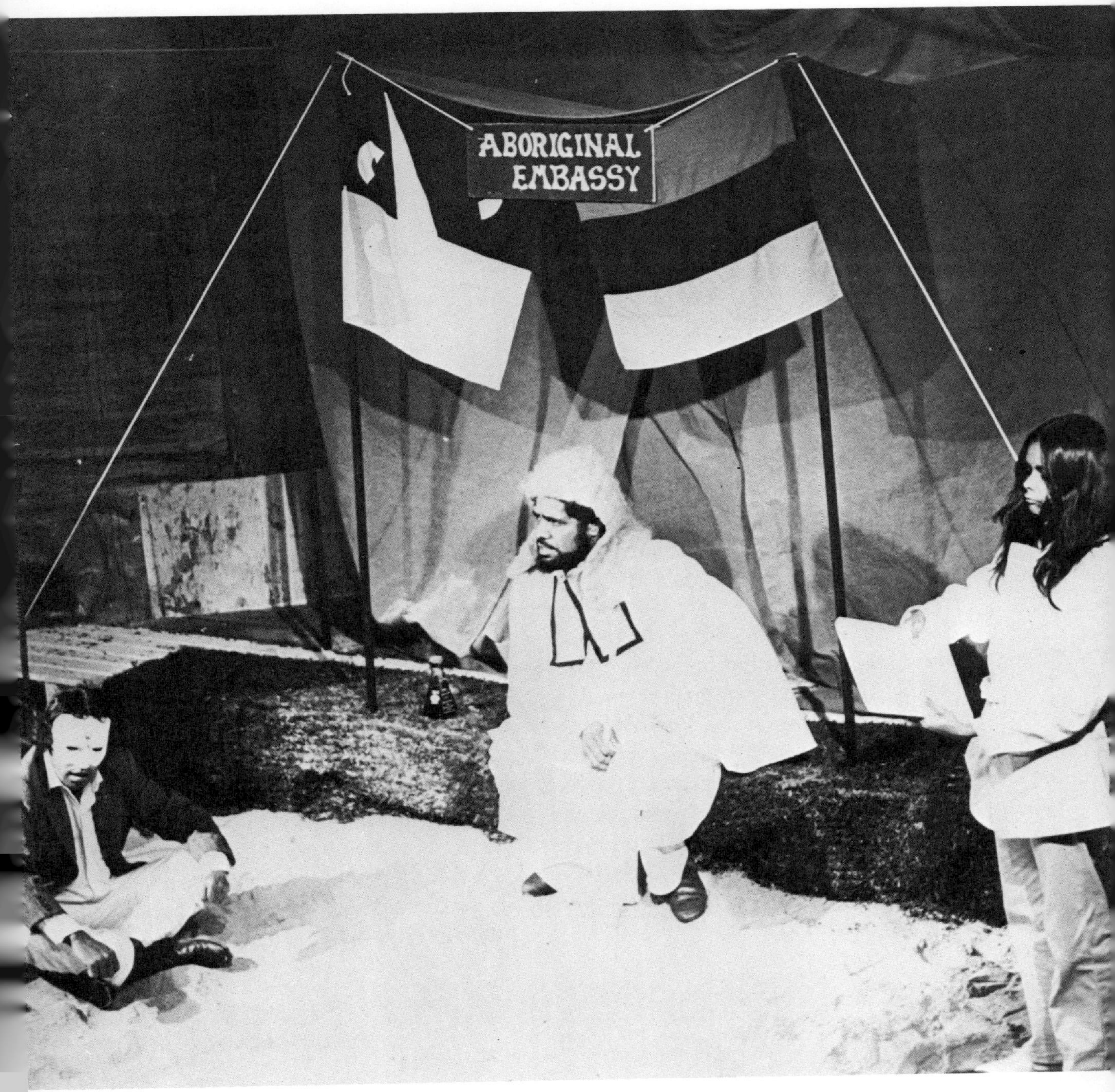
ABORIGINAL
EMBASSY

The Future

> 'Australia's treatment of her Aboriginal people will be the thing upon which the rest of the world will judge Australia and the Australians—not just now, but in the greater perspective of history.'
> —Labor Party leader Gough Whitlam, December 1972

The future of Aboriginals is important—not just for Aboriginals, but for all Australians. If relations between black and white Australians were to worsen, the results could be violent, and harmful to Australia's good name.

What will the future be? There are many different opinions. Some people are gloomy and pessimistic. They point out that despite all the changes in laws in recent years and all the extra money being spent, the housing, health and employment position of the Aboriginal people remains bad. For some Aboriginals, due to the 1975-77 economic recession and other economic factors, it has worsened. While there is more consultation, many Aboriginals feel that the basic decisions are still made by white people.

Writing in the *National Times* of 8 November, 1976 Professor Colin Tatz, an expert on Aboriginal matters, wrote:

'Aboriginal disenchantment grows in Australia: many see moderation as pointless. They perceive white doors as closed, barred and intransigent. The political system offers them nothing as a way out from down under. The vote is meaningless, except that in the long term, Aborigines may be able to elect a black majority to the Northern assembly. Aboriginal affairs continues to be a white activity: white-decided policies,

Thirty years ago, Aboriginals were seldom mentioned in the daily papers. But here, in one issue of the *Sydney Morning Herald* in 1977 (June 16) are three articles on Aboriginal issues. The articles suggest that greater attention should be paid to Aboriginal attitudes, customs and activity in the important matters of health, law, and land rights.

Changes in Aboriginal health care urged

CANBERRA. — A Government-sponsored report released yesterday has proposed that Aboriginal health care in Central Australia be handed over gradually to the local people.

It says the Departments of Health, Aboriginal Affairs and Education should withdraw from their dominant role and accept that of a supportive and advisory one.

The report was prepared by Dr Trevor Cutter for the Central Australian Aboriginal Congress with the aid of a grant of $18,000 from the previous Federal Government.

Dr Cutter, speaking at a press briefing yesterday, said the degree of chronic illness among Aboriginal children in the Alice Springs area was the worst he had ever seen.

Some of the areas he could personally compare the situation with included India, Bangladesh, and Ethiopia during the famine some years ago.

A survey carried out at the settlement of Papunya, west of Alice Springs, found that half of the elderly pensioners suffered from total blindness.

Dr Cutter said the existing health care system had clearly failed, largely because it was alien to the Aborigines.

"Imagine how a tribal Aboriginal feels when admitted to the air-conditioned, sterile corridors of the $20 million Alice Springs hospital," Dr Cutter said.

"The staff are white, they speak a foreign language, the patient's friends and relatives are kept away, the treatment is novel and possibly frightening.

"The result is a disaster."

In addition to Aborigines taking over the health delivery services, the report strongly urges that greater recognition be given to tribal healers, or ngangkaris.

Don't bury our laws, pleads Aboriginal

DARWIN. — Burrumarra, an Aboriginal elder from Arnhem Land, made a strong plea yesterday for the legal customs of the Aboriginal clans not to be "buried" by white Australians.

In a recorded submission to the Australian Law Reform Commission, Burrumarra said traditional Aboriginal law must be kept alive and strong.

"You got the law," he said, "but we got the law too.

"The law — Aboriginal laws — must stay alive and not be destroyed. Do not dig a big hole and bury them.

"Don't forget, Aboriginal people are the first people in Australia. The law should be in Arnhem Land — one of ours and one of yours," Burrumarra said.

The reform commission is looking into the extent to which the Australian legal system should recognise customary Aboriginal law.

Aboriginal land rights talks

CANBERRA. — A Federal parliamentary committee will hold discussions on Aboriginal land rights with Aboriginal communities and traditional landowners in the Northern Territory next week.

The discussions will centre on the operation of the land councils set up by the Government's Aboriginal land rights legislation last year.

laws, practices, administrations, programmes. . . . huge infusions of money solved little. . . . Aborigines remain impoverished, unemployed, discriminated against, sick. . . .'

This is the pessimistic view. But there are many people who have a more optimistic outlook. They point to the fact that in the past twenty years there have been big changes for the better. In all States except Queensland the laws which denied equality have been ended. The Federal Government has become the main body responsible for policy. The idea of 'absorbing' the Aboriginal so that he becomes an imitation white man has been abandoned. Far more money is being spent on Aboriginal housing, health and education. Large numbers of Aboriginals have become active in their own organisations and are gaining experience and training—and the main political parties agree that Aboriginals must have land rights—and the right to have a big say in deciding their own future.

If there has been so much forward movement in twenty years, the optimists say, there must be further movement forward in the future. But even the most optimistic would agree that it won't come easily. In a democratic country like Australia, any group in a difficult position can only advance itself if it exerts pressures in a number of democratic ways—not just by voting, but by lobbying, by demonstrating, through meetings, congresses, petitions, or whatever method is necessary. The pressures will sometimes be polite and friendly, sometimes more in the nature of a 'confrontation.'

Just as impoverished farmers might find it necessary to march through Sydney streets, or nurses demanding better conditions might intrude into Parliament House, so Aboriginals may have to march through Darwin streets on occasions, or assemble in Canberra, or demonstrate in other ways. But the optimists say that the changes of the last twenty years have shown that the doors are open. And they see hope in the growing realisation that Aboriginals must have a greater say.

Queensland Aboriginal Len Watson, writing in the *National Times* supplement of 1 April, 1974 sees the future as one of 'confrontation in all areas.' But he sees some hope—if white people will listen to Aboriginals. 'Black people themselves must be involved not only in the implementation of new policies regarding them, but also the policy making. There will be mistakes. You cannot expect people who have

Primary school children learning a traditional dance

been brutalised, massacred and kept as fifth-rate citizens, people ridiculed in so many ways and treated in a very racist manner, to start governing themselves and to start working out problems for themselves without failures. It takes expertise, it takes experience. Most important of all, you've got to be given room to make mistakes. White policy makers have made plenty of mistakes. . . .'

Perhaps this is the road forward—through listening more to the Aboriginals, and giving them a greater voice in their future. You who read this book will help make the road. If the right road can be found, it will be good for all Australians.

Follow-up Activities

1. Make a time chart, with the same space representing each 1000 years, to show a few of the main events of Australian history in the past 40,000 years.

2. Visit a museum and make a study of Aboriginal implements and how they are made and used.

3. Visit a museum or exhibition or shop displaying modern Aboriginal arts and handicrafts. Find out what you can about where and by whom they are made, and what story or meaning is conveyed.

4. Make a list of Aboriginal place names and what is thought to be their meaning.

5. Arrange a reading of Aboriginal stories and of poems by such Aboriginal poets as Kath Walker and Jack Davis.

6. Arrange a showing of films depicting Aboriginal life or culture.

7. Arrange the playing of recordings of Aboriginal music.

8. Invite an Aboriginal speaker to talk on some aspect of Aboriginal life.

9. Find out what you can about Aboriginal history in your particular area or in a nearby area.

Index

Aboriginal Arts Board 103
Aboriginal Embassy 93, 104
Aboriginal organisations 62, 71-75, 99-104
Aboriginal Legal Service 88, 99
Aboriginal Medical Service 99, 100-102
Aboriginal Theatre 99, 103
Aborigines Advancement League 74
Aborigines Progressive Association 62-66
Aborigines Protection and Welfare Boards 56, 62
alcohol 42, 52, 56
art 27-29, 78, 80
assimilation 53-54, 60
Association for Protection of Native Races 61
Aurukun 92

Bandler, Faith 96
Bates, Daisy 57-59
Batman, John 51
Bennelong 41-42
Blainey, Geoffrey 16, 31
Blair, Harold 77
Bonner, Senator Neville 80, 88, 104
boomerang 24-26
Bryant, Gordon 91, 94
Bungaree 76

Captain Cook 32-33, 37
cattle industry 86
characteristics of Aboriginals 10
churches, religious education 52, 54-56, 85
Collins, David 43
colonialism 37
Commonwealth programmes 81-82, 93-98
conservation 17-21
Coonamble 84
co-operation 21-22
corroborees 30
cricketers 76
Cummeragunga 63-64, 66

Darling, Governor 44
dances 30
Davis, Jack 42, 80
Day of Mourning 64
definition of Aboriginal 10
digging sticks 26
diseases introduced 37-38, 58
discrimination 86-87, 88
Dreaming, Dreamtime 29
Duncan, Alan 104
'Dying Race' theory 57-59, 81

education, Aboriginal 29, 30, 33-34, 104
education by authorities 52-53, 56
Elkin, Professor A. P. 61, 76
Embassy, Aboriginal 93, 104
employment 82, 84, 86
ethnocentrism 40

FCAATSI (Federal Council) 71-75
Ferguson, Bill 62-66
fire 19, 26
food gathering, food plants 14
fringe dwellers 73-74

games 32-34
Gilmore, Mary 18-19
Goolagong, Evonne 78
Grassby, Al 86-87
Groves, Bert 60, 62, 71
Gurindjis 90-91

health 82, 84, 85, 100-102
Hermannsburg Mission 67
housing 82, 84-85

integration 60

Kalokerinos, Dr A. 102
Kirinari 104
Kunoth, Rosalie 77-78

Labor Party 74, 81, 85, 91-94, 97
land and religion 16
land councils 94
land rights 89-92, 93
Land Rights Commission 91, 94
land taking 38-51
land trusts 92
languages 13
laws 22, 30, 61
Liberal Party 74, 91-92, 98

McLeod, Donald 69-70
Mapoon 92
massacres 45-48
meaning of 'Aboriginal' 8
Milne, G. N. 63-64
mineral rights 92, 93
missionaries 52, 54-56, 85
Moongalba 103
Mosik 78
multi-racial society 81
Murawina Child Care Centre 99
music 31
Myall Creek massacre 45, 46

Namatjira, Albert 67-70, 72
names 34-36
National Aboriginal Consultative Council 94-95
native police 46
Nicholls, Sir Douglas 37, 64, 72, 78
nomads 16, 26

origin of Aboriginals 11

paternalism 40
Patten, Jack 64, 66
Perkins, Charles 80
Phillip, Governor 38, 41
Pilbara strike 69-70
poets 79-80
poisons 27
police 46, 47, 57, 88
population 13, 49-51, 59, 82
protection policies 54-56
protest associations 62-66, 71-75

Queensland 86, 94

race theories, racism 39-41, 87
Redfern 84
referendum of 1967 74
religion, Aboriginal 16, 19, 21-22, 29, 30
resistance 45, 48
Roth, W. E. 14, 27
Roughsey, Dick 80, 103

sacred areas 19, 89, 93, 94
Saunders, Captain Reg 77
segregation 59-60, 99
sharing 21
skills 24-31
sportsmen 76, 78-79
state laws 72-73, 86, 94
stereotypes 41
Strehlow, T. G. H. 19

Tasmanian Aboriginals 51
Tatz, Professor Colin 106
Threlkeld, Rev. L. E. 54-55
Torres Strait Islanders 72
totemism 21
Tranby 103
treaties 48, 51
tribes, tribal structure 13, 22, 30
Tuckiar 61-62
Tudawali, Robert 21, 77-78

Uranium mining 92
Urbanisation 82-83

Walker, Kath 75, 79, 103
Waters, Fred 66
Watson, Len 108-109
Weipa 89, 92
white backlash 96
Woodward Commission 91, 94
woolgrowing 44-45
Woomera 24
Wylie 76

Yandy 69, 70
Yirawala 28-29, 78
Yirrkala 86, 89-90